THE CANADIAN CLASS STRUCTURE

McGRAW-HILL RYERSON SERIES IN CANADIAN SOCIOLOGY

GENERAL EDITOR — LORNE TEPPERMAN
Department of Sociology
University of Toronto

DEMOGRAPHIC BASES OF CANADIAN SOCIETY
Warren Kalbach and Wayne McVey

A STATISTICAL PROFILE OF CANADIAN SOCIETY
Daniel Kubat and David Thornton

IDEOLOGICAL PERSPECTIVES ON CANADA
M. Patricia Marchak

SOCIAL MOBILITY IN CANADA
Lorne Tepperman

THE CANADIAN CLASS STRUCTURE
Dennis Forcese

CANADIAN SOCIETY IN HISTORICAL PERSPECTIVE
S. D. Clark

FORTHCOMING

ETHNIC GROUP RELATIONS IN CANADA
Wsevolod Isajiw

SOCIAL CHANGE IN CANADA
Lorna Marsden

THE DISREPUTABLE PLEASURES
John Hagan

The Canadian Class Structure

Dennis Forcese

Carleton University

McGRAW-HILL RYERSON LIMITED

Toronto   Montreal   London   New York
Sydney   Johannesburg   Mexico   Panama
Düsseldorf   Singapore   New Delhi
Kuala Lumpur   São Paulo

THE CANADIAN CLASS STRUCTURE

ISBN 0-07-082265-4

3 4 5 6 7 8 9 10 AP 10 9 8 7

Printed and bound in Canada

Contents

Acknowledgements

Although they have had no direct hand in this book, and certainly share no responsibility for its inadequacies, I wish to thank three former graduate students, Wallace Clement, Sid Gilbert, and Hugh McRoberts. We passed seemingly inconsequential hours of casual and not so casual conversation, the results of which have somehow lingered on. Believing in distributive justice, I like to think that our exchanges were equitable, but I suspect that I have learned more from them than they from me. I sincerely hope that they approve of this book. May they always have fond memories of Carleton University's "golden age". My thanks to Barbara Cameron and her trusty borrowed typewriter, for rescuing me and my messy manuscript.

Preface

This book is an overview of what is known about social stratification in Canada. The extensive list of references is indicative of my attempt to integrate the pertinent information. The result is a rather selective introduction to the many aspects of institutionalized inequality in Canada.

I have not attempted to write a work of theory in the ambitious sense, but simply a presentation and interpretation of my perceptions of the facts of the Canadian social class structure. Certainly this is not a work that attempts to affiliate itself with or regurgitate any particular "classic" theory. I think it eclectic, rather than a contrived effort at making a Karl Marx, a Max Weber, or even a Ludwig Gumplowicz fit the Canadian circumstance. I have been accused by some colleagues, perhaps not in jest, of advocating sociological parricide. There is truth in the charge, not that I wish to deny the insight and guidance of the "classics", but that I weary of repeated classical exegesis. So, though I deal in first concepts, assumptions, and findings, and though alternatives and their origins are summarized in the text, this is definitely not a book of great names revisited.

It may well be the case that this is but an elaborate rationalization for my own mal-integrated approach to the study of social stratification; that is, of course, for the reader to judge. I am satisfied that it has not been an excuse to avoid the articulation of personal values or goals regarding social stratification. There are theoretically derived premises explicitly presented in the book: the non-inevitability of social class stratification; the existence of class conflict in Canada; and the desirability of political action to the goal of a genuinely egalitarian society.

I should point out that my emphasis differs from the pure power and stratification school of analysis, best represented by John Porter's *The Vertical Mosaic*. I am of the view that Porter's work remains the single outstanding contribution to the sociological study of Canadian society, and for that reason alone I would feel foolish in spending any more time than I do in summarizing some of his already well-known findings and interpretations. Instead, I have chosen to emphasise non-elites in Canadian society. Conceding the economic basis of power, I am interested in the relations of Canadians to the fact of concentrated wealth and power, and of the relations of non-elite Canadians with one another. Particularly, the nature of class awareness and resentment and possible bases of class action and social change have preoccupied me, as much or more than an exploration of the rigidities of institutionalized inequality. I do no expect that social change will emanate from the elite or ruling class; rather, if we are to have change, we must expect it from the hitherto "smug" middle-class majority, and from *organized* industrial and rural workers. This said, I confess that I am not yet certain whether it stands as an expression of pessimism or of optimism.

DPF
Ottawa

Editor's Introduction

The publication of Dennis Forcese's book on social stratification in Canada is an important event in its own right, but it has special significance for the McGraw-Hill Ryerson Series in Canadian sociology. Within the series, this book completes a trilogy, each book concerned with the structure of inequality in Canada. However, the three books in question — this one, Professor Marchak's *Ideological Perspective on Canada*, and my own book, *Social Mobility in Canada* — each approach the study of inequality with a somewhat different purpose and viewpoint. The trilogy is therefore something of a comprehensive introduction to inequality in Canada and an implicit debate between differing approaches.

Professor Marchak, author of *Ideological Perspectives on Canada*, has as her purpose the analysis of competing ideologies about Canadian society held by Canadians themselves. These ideologies organize people's understanding of existing inequality and serve to legitimate particular courses of social action or, even, inaction. Professor Marchak shows how specific ideologies may be more or less appropriate to particular moments in Canadian history and argues for a radical rethinking of how Canada is or ought to be organized. The second book, *Social Mobility in Canada*, is less concerned with inequality of condition than with inequality of opportunity in Canada. It analyzes not ideological formulations but rather the commonplace factors affecting the attainment of "success" in our own society. While this book contains some discussion of intergenerational and group mobility in Canada and other industrial societies, far more attention is given to the organization of careers within a nonegalitarian society such as our own.

Professor Forcese's *Canadian Class Structure* provides us with excellent up-to-date information on how much inequality is found in Canada today and what practical and ideological matters impede changing this situation. Inequality of condition in Canada has many bases, including educational attainment, ethnic origin, sex, and geographic or regional location. The book discusses how these individual characteristics are translated into hierarchical statuses within a system that has proved pervasive and enduring. A final chapter ties together the themes of socio-economic organization, inequality of condition, and class conflict in a way that provides us with insight into the future of Canadian society and, additionally, brings us back full circle to the issues of ideological perspective dealt with by Professor Marchak at greater length. It is impossible to summarize this book about stratification in a way that would do justice to its content and exposition; so I shall leave off at this point.

I close by reminding the reader that all scholarship represents a debate between contending approaches, as well as a search for better information and more elegant formulations of a given approach. The reader is therefore enjoined to participate in this debate by reading and discussing the trilogy of books I have named, of which Professor Forcese's volume is an excellent representative.

L.T.

1
STRATIFICATION IN PERSPECTIVE

The Ubiquity of Inequality

Mankind has never wanted for utopian conceptions of society. Recorded history offers us repeated instances of men dreaming of some better form of social existence wherein man would live in perfect and fulfilling harmony with man. Such utopias have always had to come to grips with inequality. Some thinkers have done so with an image of the best and most fulfilling form of inequality, such as Plato's emphasis upon a society of communal property, yet governed by an enlightened ruling class. Similarly, Auguste Comte envisaged a socialist society guided by social engineers or sociologist priests. Others, such as in the early Christian tradition, have resisted notions of necessary distinctions among men, and have insisted upon a fundamental equality. Thomas More, who gave us the word "utopia", writing in 1516 argued for a communal ownership, ideally guided by Christian love and brotherhood.

The 18th-century liberal ideology of the new American republic also projected a utopian image. It was oriented about an equality of opportunity founded on a society of free and independent property holders. This equality was constitutionally guaranteed and celebrated. Yet, though the object of this liberal sentiment was a goal less difficult than full equality of condition, in the sense of only guaranteeing equal opportunity to compete for unequal rewards, the United States has failed to realize its utopian inspiration. The opportunity for wealth, as wealth itself, has proved to be inheritable, such that each generation of Americans begins its quest for the "American dream" from enormously variable starting points.

Another utopian image that continues to intrigue contemporary idealists and social critics is that of Karl Marx. The Marxist dream was of a classless society wherein men realized their potential as human beings and no longer suffered the inequities and humiliations of inferior status and benefits. For Marx, industrial society such as that of 19th-century England was bourgeois class society, a system in which the *bourgeoisie* or owners of property ruled and exploited the *proletariat* or wage slaves. Eventually, Marx reasoned, the vast proletariat would develop a *class consciousness*, recognize the common misery of their lives, and act as an effective political force to violently overthrow the bourgeoisie. Private property, the basis of wealth and

1

power, would be abolished. Each man would work for himself, producing according to his skills and inclination and receiving according to his needs. Human society would have evolved to its highest form, and humankind would be fulfilled. (Marx, 1947; 1955; Anderson, 1974.)

The power of such an image is obvious — as obvious as the appeal of Christianity. Yet, despite dedicated converts, despite nations formally committed to Marxist goals, somehow the goal of perfect equality has proved elusive, and Marxist nations find themselves coping with inequalities that seem to be becoming increasingly rigid. (Bottomore, 1965: 47-60; Parkin, 1972: 137-159; Djilas, 1957.)

Some sociological theorists believe the failure inevitable, for they believe that the hierarchical differentiation or inequality of men in society to be inevitable. For example, Kingsley Davis and Wilbert Moore wrote of the *functional necessity* of some form of differentiation or stratification. (Davis and Moore, 1942.) In order to survive, they argued, societies must see to the performance of certain functionally necessary tasks. And since these tasks cannot be left to chance performance, and since they are not all equally attractive, a society must contain practices that ensure that persons are assigned specific roles and motivated to perform them. An unequal system of rewards realizes such *role allocation*, argued Davis and Moore, and motivates the performance of the requisite behaviour associated with such roles. In their view the forms of stratification might differ widely, and the variation in rewards might be extreme or slight, but some variation must necessarily come to pass if a society is to persist as a viable unit.

The functionalist view makes much of the difficulties of role allocation and of motivation, assuming that the performance of socially relevant tasks is dependent upon pay-off for the performers. Gouldner (1970) suggests that functionalism is a variation on the theme of 19th-century utilitarianism, in that it takes culturally relative definitions of the utility or the value of specific roles and tasks to be indicative of some functional necessity. In contrast to functionalist emphasis upon system maintenance, Marx made light of the problems of social organization and what historically has been human maximization of reward. On the one hand, functionalists suggest that rewards, and by implication, material rewards, must be unequally allocated or human society is impossible. On the other hand, Marxists suggest that society will develop to a stage wherein human beings can divest themselves of any inclination to differentially distribute wealth.

Sociologists other than the functionalists have argued the inevitability of inequality. For example, Gaetano Mosca (1939) was of the view that there would always be a ruling class because society, with its complexity, requires that there be political organization. Thus, there must be inequalities in power. And since man is self-seeking, power will acquire privilege or wealth. (Mosca, 1939; Lenski, 1966.) Similarly, in 1911 Robert Michels (1958) published his study of the German Social Democratic Party and concluded that there obtains an "iron law of oligarchy". Because of specialized tasks, requiring expertise and the expenditure of time and effort, inevitably a minority within any human organization will come to monopolize decision making or power. The masses will tend to opt out, from disinterest, lack of information, and because of the sheer cost in time and effort, and those already making decisions will consolidate their positions of power and advantage. (Michels, 1958.)

Taking a similar tone, the contemporary Canadian sociologist John Porter (1965) suggests that the highly complex and specialized nature of modern society has necessitated complex and specialized government and corporate organization. Those making decisions in these government and economic organizations have enormous power. Unlike the American sociologist C. Wright Mills (1959), who deemed such persons "the power elite", Porter does not believe that these powerful act in full consensus; they are in competition and conflict as well as in collusion. But they do rule society. (Porter, 1965: 22-28.)

Porter is suggesting that power is a means to the exploitation of property and resources and is therefore crucial. In a somewhat similar fashion, Dahrendorf (1959) offered what he believed a necessary modification of Marxism, and stressed that in modern societies there is a basic struggle for political power as the basis of differential control of property and wealth. Neither property nor power were the complete basis of inequality. Writing early in the 20th century, Weber (1946; 1947; 1958) also stressed non-economic considerations. Weber noted that persons distinguished among themselves by prestige as well as by power and economic possession. Lenski agrees, and speaks of prestige, power and privilege. (Lenski, 1966.) Thus, many sociologists today take the view that there are three principal dimensions of stratification: the honorific (prestige), the political (power), and the economic (wealth).

The Weberian three-fold distinction suggests that stratification is complex rather than merely a matter of economic differentiation. It further implies that full equality may fail to materialize even when there is equal distribution of wealth. Human history contains examples of societies that approximate the Marxist ideal, insofar as they avoid disparities in material reward or wealth. Yet there is no convincing example of a viable human society in which there has not been some differentiation in prestige and in power. That is, even where a society has had few persisting differences in the material possessions of its members, these societies have been characterized by distinct and recognized differences in the prestige or honour assigned to people and in the power or ability of people to control the behaviour of others. These minimal differences in prestige and power have derived from individual characteristics or skills. By implication, they are awarded individuals in recognition or reward of their behaviour and use of skills to the perceived advantage of the collectivity. But honour and power also have been inherited across generations, such that individuals come to enjoy benefits irrespective of their own achievements or contributions to society. Even in the simplest of societies such inheritance is not altogether avoided. We can illustrate inequality of prestige and power, in the absence of inequality of wealth, by considering very simple human societies.

Hunting and Gathering Societies

In simple hunting and gathering societies, we have an example of the most rudimentary level of human social organization. Peoples at this level of social existence are literally dependent for their existence upon foodstuffs that they collect from the natural environment, the items that women gather and dig up and the animals men bring home from the hunt. There is no cultivation of plants or herding of animals. Nor, with the exception of some peoples who occupy lush and abundant environments, are there permanent settlements. The small bands of people, 10 to 30 in size, are nomadic; they must move with the seasons to secure their subsistence. And there is typically no accumulation of wealth; the absence of an economic surplus is a distinguishing feature. (Lenski, 1966; 94-116.) A conspicuous exception, the Kwakiutl of what is now British Columbia, were able to accumulate considerable wealth; yet people's ranks were distinguished not by the accumulation *per se*, but by reciprocal exchanges of property, or in the extreme "rivalry potlatches", by offering resources for consumption or destruction. Thus the *potlatch* was a means of establishing and "validating" relations of social status. (Druker, 1965; 55-66.)

The usual hunting and gathering society is aptly described as communal. As in the Eskimo bands of Canada before contact with Europeans, it is unquestioningly accepted that there be full co-operation and sharing. Without necessarily recognizing the consequence, this communal ownership and consumption, administered through the organization of the extended family, serves to secure the maintenance and security of the collectivity. No matter which hunter is responsible for the kill, for example, the meat will be distributed through the band, along kinship lines, until everyone has a share.

There is a limited technology, such as pointed digging sticks, spears, bows and arrows, and no control over the production of foodstuffs, except that vested in knowledge of plants and animals and skill in obtaining their yield. Thus, essentially hunting and gathering peoples remain subject to the fluctuations of climate, much more than agriculturalists, for their yield is modest and is not preserved or stored. The life of a hunting and gathering band is thereby harsh and precarious, co-operation is essential, and deviance intolerable. There are no legal paraphernalia, however, such as we are familiar with to ensure minimal conformity. Laws are not formally articulated, nor are persons designated as responsible for ensuring obedience to such laws. The very isolation of such peoples, lacking exposure to alternate societies and ways of life, ensures a basic uniformity of behaviour, for there has been a uniformity of socialization. That is, unlike the case of large complex societies such as our own, the members of a hunting and gathering band will face few options in life. There is a simple division of labour by gender and age, and people all learn the expected behaviours. Where deviance does occur, the small size of the band, and the norms of kinship authority, are effective controls within the parameters of socialization. And ultimately, there are the fearful sanctions of ostracism and banishment for persistent or serious offences. Given the harshness of the environment and the need for co-operation, banishment becomes a virtual death sentence. In some societies, such as the Eskimo, execution is the ultimate penalty, and is the responsibility of kin and the immediate band.

Because of the rudimentary level of existence, there is little social differentiation in such societies. There are certainly no social classes, in the sense of social classes as strata of individuals within a society differentiated by wealth. But there is some differentiation; more important, there is some hierarchical or vertical differentiation, specifically by power and prestige, and this hierarchical differentiation to some extent persists across generations, for it is inherited. It thereby constitutes what we take to be a minimal social stratification.

At the most elementary level, we find differences in ascribed social position related to birth and biological maturation, and in turn normatively defined in relation to the elementary division of labour. Thus, for example, women gather foodstuffs and men hunt. In addition, not only are the roles different, they and their occupants are valued differently; it is at this point that hierarchical differentiation occurs. Women, for example, characteristically enjoy a lesser prestige and power than do men; children less than adults. But moreover, in addition to such inequality by ascription, some individuals demonstrate valued skills or attributes relatively lacking in others. Such persons are respected and assume greater prestige, and their suggestions and initiatives are valued. They have greater influence than other members of the band; they become leaders. Sometimes this leadership is formalized; sometimes, as among some Eskimo, there is little formalization — no conception, for example, of chieftainship. (Weyer, 1932; 210-214.) But insofar as these skilled individuals elicit deference and others comply with their directions, a leadership status is distinguished from the rank and file members of the band. For example, the skilled hunter is extremely important to the survival of the band, and his skills are recognized and his advice, at least in hunting, is respected. There will usually not be laws or norms requiring compliance with such advice and punishments for failure to comply; but insofar as an individual has valuable skills, the probability of compliance is great, because it is in the interest of the collectivity. Thus, individuals come to be distinguished on the basis of their contributions to the group, or as Lenski put it, we find "functional inequality". (Lenski, 1966: 105.) Other skills than those related to hunting may be recognized, such as the mystical and practical skills of a *shaaman* or medicine man to whom people will turn for advice and assistance. (Lenski, 1966: 100-101.) If the skills of hunter and spiritual/medical leader coincide in a single individual, that individual may become very powerful indeed, for he is granted the voluntary compliance of other members of the band.

In stressing differentiation by skills, we suggest a fluid system of inequality, relating to individual qualities and achievement. But such skills are not entirely a function of the luck of the biological draw. In some part they can be accounted for by socialization, and are thereby socially inherited. The sons of the hunter, or the *shaaman*, are more likely to learn the skills of the father than are other members of the band. That is, the parent will impart information to his sons, while the other members of the band will tend to expect that the child of a skilful person will have inherited these skills, thereby generating a self-fulfilling prophecy. Thus, although a biologically determined capacity is necessary, it is important to realize that the opportunity to shape such a capacity is also important, and it is more likely to be shaped in a manner consistent with existing differentiation.

Because skilled individuals have the opportunity to pass on skills to those whom they choose, whether their own children or others, and other members of the band are inclined to expect certain behaviour from persons associated with those of recognized skill, the son of a great hunter and leader is given greater opportunity to establish a similar status than would other members of the band. This is but a short step, then, from establishing hereditary leadership, which in some instances does become formally institutionalized. The son of a leader or headman is given the benefit of the doubt, and often has to disprove himself to lose status rather than prove himself to secure leadership status.

The point of this description is that in the most simple form of human social organization some hierarchical differentiation exists. This differentiation constitutes minimal stratification, insofar as it is inherited across generations. It is not stratification of a complex sort, for the role differentiation and population size are slight in keeping with the slight technology that can support only a small population. Nor, for the same reasons and in the absence of differential wealth, do we find ranked collectivities or aggregates that we could view as classes. But some individuals are distinguished from others in prestige and in power — women from men, children from adults, the elderly from the vigorous adults, and the skilled from the unskilled. In this most egalitarian of known human societies, perfect equality or the complete absence of stratification in its broadest sense is not realized. The inequality is not due to some innate and sinister drive to power or will to dominate or greed, but is *the product of a collectivity organized for survival.*

Minimal Stratification

If one contrasts such simple hunting and gathering societies to modern industrialized Canada, we can perhaps be less incredulous when we encounter contemporary stratification. The hunting and gathering peoples are small in number and accumulate virtually no possessions. They have a minimal division of labour and only kinship organization. Yet differentiation by prestige and power occurs. Little wonder that it occurs, therefore, in more complex societies, with large populations, a considerable technology and variations in skill, a vast range of durable material possessions, and a mass-communications ability that renders visible many alternate ways of life, such that conformity becomes problematic and the implementation of power to regulate deviance a major social task.

Existing knowledge of all forms of society or levels of social organization suggests that *some hierarchical social differentiation or stratification has always existed* (Lenski, 1966) and, given the minimal subtle variations in influence and prestige that characterize human relations, some hierarchical differentiation and even a fragile inheritance is probably inevitable. We stress that this is a far different statement than it would be to say that class society is inevitable. And it is certainly not an endorsement of any given degree or kind of differentiation or inequality. Indeed, to be perfectly clear, we are of the view that differentiation in a complex society could theoretically approximate that of a hunting and gathering society, in that we find no empirical or theoretical basis suggesting the necessity, as opposed to the convenience and near ubiquity, of inheritable economic differences. Minimal stratification by prestige and by influence or power is ineradicable. Differentiation in power and prestige is a function of interaction and social organization, and the more complex that interaction and organization, the greater such differentiation. Unfortunately, because money or essential commodities are visible and quantifiable, where prestige and power are not, the more complex the tasks performed in a society, the greater the probability of monetary or material differentiation. This is simply to say that economic reward, though not necessary to motivate behaviour, is convenient. But it is not functionally necessary, however practical or expedient. Even if utilized it is not necessary that economic reward be differentially assigned to persons, especially to the extent of massive disparities, nor is it necessary that material reward be passed on to heirs.

Thus, without resorting to the language or the assumptions of functionalist theory, or the assumption of necessary economic differentiation, or the endorsement of large disparities among peoples, or the institutionalization of such disparities over time and across generations, we do assert that some minimal degree of social stratification is inevitable. But what is highly variable is the nature and the extremity of stratification systems. Stratification as we find it, in contemporary Canada, is not inevitable. Nor, to make a very personal statement of value, is it to be condoned. Rather, it can be explained, understood, and changed. But whatever the changes and however desirable they might be viewed, some stratification will persist. *What is crucial, because it is of enormous impact upon human lives, and because theoretically it is remediable and not inevitable, is economic stratification or class stratification.*

Minimally Stratified Society: The Hutterites

Recent history has witnessed numerous attempts to realize the goal of the economically egalitarian society, and they have typically collapsed far short of the ideal. A dramatic exception that illustrates our thesis of minimally inevitable stratification in the absence of class is that of the Hutterite communal colonies, scattered throughout the provinces of Manitoba, Saskatchewan, and Alberta.

The Hutterites are an Anabaptist religious sect, motivated by a conception of Christian community and equality. Founded by Joseph Hutter, they fled from Germany to Russia during the European counter-Reformation of the 17th century. Persecution by Czarist regimes over Hutterite resistance to conscription prompted the Hutterite migration to North America. Colonies were founded in North Dakota and Minnesota, but more settled in the prairie provinces of Canada. (Peters, 1965; Bennett, 1967; Bennett, 1969.)

There they have literally prospered and multiplied. And they have done so without compromising with the secular society surrounding them. They are unlike the adherents of the other Anabaptist sects, the Mennonites and the Amish, who have, with few exceptions, abandoned any communal organization and whose members have largely been assimilated into the larger North American society. They maintain a rural existence segregated from the stimuli of modern urban Canada.

The Hutterites live in colonies of a maximum size of about one hundred. When a colony exceeds that number, a new colony is established, for until recently, land for expansion in the Canadian West had been readily available. There are continuous challenges to continued expansion of Hutterite colonies, for as perceived by other farmers, and to some extent in fact, their communal organization, pooling of resources, and modest consumption permits them the capital to expand where the individual farmer (as opposed to corporate agriculturalists) may not. In addition, the Hutterites are largely self-sufficient, and as their opponents stress, they spend little money in surrounding communities. Their major expenditures are on new machinery, and these are not purchases usually made from local merchants. In Alberta, where the majority of the Hutterite population — about 40,000 — live, the government legislated (although subsequently removed) limitations upon Hutterite expansion. (Russell, 1974.)

The Hutterites are extremely efficient agriculturalists; they employ the most modern techniques and machinery, and because of their collective organization, they can afford such modern products of technology. But the agricultural output is for the collectivity, not individuals. The Hutterites emphasize "all things common". People dress alike, in basic black, with modest colour tone variations in items of clothing such as a man's shirt or a woman's bandana. Women are readily recognized by their "mother-hubbard" dresses and bandana-covered heads; the men by their black suits or work-clothing, and beards if married. Each family has private quarters, but the adults eat together in a communal dining hall, segregated by sex. The hall also doubles as a place of worship, for there are no churches. The children eat together, separate from the adults, under the care and supervision of the Hutterite teacher and his wife.

Individuals have virtually no possessions. The uniform clothing and prohibition against accumulating wealth or items of adornment are intended to minimize differences, much as is intended by the uniformity of dress in Mao's China. A young unmarried girl might have a few items of clothing and keepsakes in her hope chest, but little else.

The Hutterite form of organization is sustained by the segregation of the colony members from outside contact, especially during childhood, and by the religious ideology. A factor characteristically missing in other similar communal communities that have failed has been a common ideological allegiance learned in the absence of alternative conceptions of social life. The Hutterite children are rigorously socialized, and they, as well as the adults, are physically segregated from the outside world. There are no books, radios, magazines, or television sets — except sometimes in the quarters of the elected leader of the colony, the preacher.

But though they are able to maintain this egalitarian structure, it cannot be said that there is no differentiation. There are, for example, the minimal differences derived of ascribed characteristics — i.e., sex and age. Certain roles are defined as suitable for women, and others for men. A woman is excluded from much of the labour involved in cultivation or ranching, but is responsible for cleaning, cooking, and mending. A woman could never be a preacher. Similarly, age demands respect, and only with maturity can one marry.

Moreover, beyond an elementary division of labour by age or gender, a related differentiation is the extent to which different roles among the males demand greater skills and vary in prestige. Thus, of crucial importance to the colony are the positions of German teacher and of preacher. In addition, there are church elders, a colony boss, and farm boss. These persons are respected, and they make decisions and can command compliance. Thus, although material items are held in common, there is differentiation along the dimensions of prestige and power. Thereby, in a rudimentary sense, there is a hierarchical differentiation. That this differentiation constitutes a stratification system is so to the extent that it is inheritable across generations. It seems to be true that, as in hunting and gathering societies, there is an inheritance of skills by virtue of socialization. Children to some extent do acquire the skills and the reputation of their parents, thereby aiding later election to influential positions. But this inheritance lacks formalization and legitimation, and rather, is defined as ideologically undesirable. In a precise sense, stratification exists, but it is remarkably slight, especially in contrast to a society such as our own.

Even the Hutterites fall short of the perfectly egalitarian society. But it is an economically egalitarian society. As in hunting and gathering societies, material wealth is shared equally, even though people are differentiated by prestige and power, which in human relations never seem to be equally distributed. However, unlike hunting and gathering societies, the Hutterites have realized their economic equality or classlessness while existing well above a subsistence level. They are a prosperous society, but the distribution of wealth is uniform among the members of the society. There are enormous institutional obstacles, but we stress that theoretically any society could similarly function in the absence of gross material differentiation — even Canadian society.

Forms of Complex Stratification

We have been using as our definition of stratification the notion that there must be persisting or inherited hierarchical differentiation in possessions, prestige, or power. Usually the three dimensions are coincident. Within this broad definition, it is possible to distinguish different forms of stratification, such as "class stratification" in Canada.

The institutionalized inequalities found in societies are not identical in organization.The extent of disparities in wealth, for example, vary from society to society, as do the disparities in prestige and in power. In some societies the extremes of wealth and poverty extend over a broad range; in others the range is relatively modest. In some societies, such as in pre-industrial or agrarian societies, we find a marked polarization between a very rich minority of the population and the mass of the population, largely a rural peasantry. Wealth, power, and prestige are concentrated, and there is no significant middle stratum. This is in contrast to industrialized societies, where, although one can still point to extremes of wealth and poverty, the majority of the population have historically constituted a middle stratum, enjoying a standard of life far superior to the impoverished masses of agrarian societies.

Whatever the precise composition of the inequality, it is important to realize that it is a structured thing, very resistant to change. In sociological terms, it is *institutionalized*; that is, persisting through inherited organization and learning or socialization.

The variations in stratification systems include not only the extent and distribution of wealth, but the degree to which the stratification is rigid or closed, as opposed to open or "permeable". (Svalastoga, 1965: 40.) Some are more rigid than others. Some permit greater opportunity for an individual to increase his wealth or power and prestige — i.e., greater opportunity for upward *social mobility*. Conversely, such open societies would also feature greater opportunity for downward social mobility. Such societies would depend to a greater extent upon individual achievements rather than upon inheritance; an individual achieves a rank or social status (*achieved status*) as opposed to inheriting or having ascribed to him a social status (*ascribed status*).

All complex societies offer some opportunity for mobility, but no complex society excludes rank by ascription or inheritance. Mobility opportunities are greater in industrialized societies than in traditional or contemporary non-industrialized societies. In that relative sense, industrial societies are open rather than closed societies.

Open societies, such as Canada's, have generally been class societies, in that mobility has been measured against the criterion of wealth. The boundaries between these classes are indistinct and not formalized, but they represent obvious variations in prestige, power, and above all, income or wealth. But because these strata are not formally sanctioned in law or custom, people may not have a clear conception or conciousness of belonging to a class, in the sense of an awareness of a commonality of situation and interests. Such an awareness is far less problematic in rigid stratification systems.

Estate

In traditional societies, distinctions by strata were more apparent. A person owned property and possessed wealth or he did not. A person had formal rank, usually hereditary, or he did not. Societies characterized by formal demarcation of strata are significantly different from class societies, precisely because the differentiation is legitimated, that is, viewed as right and proper, sanctioned by tradition and often by law. Some of the clearer examples are to be found in mediaeval Europe. For example, feudal England was a society in which there existed three distinguishable sectors: the aristocracy, the clergy, and the common people. These *estates* were legally recognized. Such legal differentiation distinguishes an estate from a class society. Each estate was itself stratified, but by law the aristocracy comprised the privileged minority of society, the hereditary landowners. Principally by the size of landholding, the nobility was itself stratified, and most significantly owed allegiance to a king. The commoners made up the peasant mass of society, and also included a slight number of craftsmen and tradesmen resident in the towns. The rural peasantry were bound to local lords and confined to the land they worked.

These distinctions were hereditary. Mobility, or achieved status, while not unknown, was not the norm. The church was a principle means of mobility, for given vows of celibacy, the clergy were dependent upon recruitment. By entering the church a common man could improve his status, for the church transcended both the aristocracy and the peasantry. Although the more prominent churchmen were normally members of the aristocracy, and themselves important landowners, people could achieve high ranks in the church despite being born to a very modest status. (Mayer and Buckley, 1969: 33-38.) A famous example from English history is that of Thomas Beckett, a merchant's son who became Archbishop of Canterbury with a power that threatened the king's.

Another historical example of estate society may be taken from Canadian history, in the case of New France. The hereditary nobility, or seigneurs, were the large landholders, and their serfs or habitants were under legal obligation to perform specified services. The clergy of the Roman Catholic Church shared in the political administration of this New France. With the British conquest, the legal nature of this feudal system was broken, although its outline lived on in land distribution and community organization. The Catholic Church, controlling educational opportunities and land, as well as religious ideology, persisted in its dominating influence well into the 20th century. From the outset, the frontier as well as the church provided opportunities for social mobility. But as the frontier gradually closed after the British conquest of New France, Quebec society settled into the stable pattern of small rural land holdings, which persist to the present in rural Quebec.

Castes

Even more rigid than estate societies are caste societies. The best example is that of traditional India; despite changes since Indian independence, even today the Indian caste distinctions survive. A *caste* is a religiously sanctioned stratum into which an individual is bound for life. Each caste is associated with an occupational role, certain norms of behaviour, and specified privileges. For example, the superior caste in traditional Indian society, in the Hindu community, was the priesthood (Brahmans). Next in standing were the warriors (Kshatryias). The third caste consisted of merchants, craftsmen, and peasants (Vaisyas). Lastly were those performing manual labour and acting as servants for the three superior castes (Sudras). Indians themselves came to distinguish several thousands of castes, many of them peculiar to local areas and associated with some specific and hereditary occupation. In 1901, the Indian census reported 2,378 such castes. (Barber, 1957: 80.) In turn, each such caste was divided into sub-castes. (Mayer and Buckely, 1969: 30-33; Barber, 1958: 80-81.) But each was viewed as inviolate, with the expectation that an individual must conform to his caste requirements or suffer the penalty, after death, of reincarnation in an inferior caste. Or as punishment in one's lifetime, one might be relegated to *outcaste* status, popularly known as the "untouchables" or the "unclean", contact with whom by caste members required subsequent acts of purification. Barber (1937: 81) reports that in 1931 one-fifth of the Indian population, or 50 million people, were outcastes.

The caste system has proved remarkably persistent, having survived wave after wave of immigrating peoples and conquests, most recently British control of the Indian subcontinent. With independence, Gandhi moved promptly to declare caste distinctions illegal, and today there are opportunities for mobility, often in government, and deliberate attempts to extend education to all castes, including the outcastes. But the awareness of caste distinctions and the traditional definition of appropriate behaviour persists, with new castes and caste functions growing up to meet the government's attempts to introduce modernity to India. Particularly at the local village level, India, overwhelmingly rural, still finds itself characterized by caste distinctions (often reinforced by ethnic and religious distinctions), and the persistence of what is perhaps history's most complex and elaborate system of institutionalized inequality.

Class

The preceding descriptions of estate and caste societies are grossly simplified. Within estates or castes there are considerable differences, such that each itself comprises a hierarchy of many strata. But they are fundamentally distinguished from class societies in that they are clearly and visibly stratified, as sanctioned or legitimated in custom, law, and religion. In class societies, such clear-cut strata and formal legitimation are absent, and to some degree repudiated as morally offensive. In a sense, the stratification is more subtle and less rigid, in that upward mobility or movement from stratum to stratum is accepted and, in fact, encouraged. Relatively, class societies are open societies, and estate and caste societies are closed. But class advantages affecting the class membership of subsequent generations are passed on through the family.

Classes are aggregates of persons distinguished principally by wealth and income. Additionally, as we have previously noted, in class societies people are distinguished by power, and by prestige and style of life, usually correlated with wealth, and comprising what some sociologists speak of as status groups or status communities. (Weber, 1958; Stub, 1972.) In large part, inherited wealth aside, one's occupation is the key to one's class and the class membership of a dependent. Classes are not formally demarcated, and the boundaries are fluid. But they do represent distinctive shared or common positions of relative privilege, and that privilege is inherited, whether directly as wealth or as opportunity to acquire wealth.

Measuring Social Class

Unlike the legal and religious definitions of estate and caste societies which are taught succeeding generations who inherit them, the strata, or classes, that make up the stratification systems of contemporary societies are difficult to identify precisely. This is particularly true of modern industrialized societies as contrasted to developing societies, for the role differentiation or division of labour is all the more elaborate. There are no formal or legal labels that distinguish a lower class from a middle class or an upper class in modern Canada. Rather, there are many imperfect indicators of class membership that Canadians more or less explicitly respond to and that the researcher can use, albeit somewhat arbitrarily.

The number of strata the social scientist distinguishes is arbitrary, as are the cutting points distinguishing one stratum from another. They are a matter of judgement and definition, as when, for example, one states that the boundary between the lower class and the middle class is an income of $10,000. But they are not merely sociological inventions. Not just some scientists, but most Canadians, even while at the same time denying the reality of classes, will vaguely distinguish strata, such as lower, middle, and upper class, and we almost all have some understanding of the kind of people to whom these labels refer, although we usually do not go about precisely designating class characteristics and boundaries.

Some researchers, such as W. Lloyd Warner, make much finer distinctions. In his community studies, Warner at times speaks of strata within each of the lower, middle, upper-middle, and upper class. And he found that people were able to make such distinctions; in particular, people were able to make fine distinctions within their own broad stratum, as when lower-class individuals distinguished the "shiftless" from the good worker. The upper class (I) consists of persons of wealth, and wealth that extends over several generations; these are established families, the "silk stockings". The upper-middle class (II) consists of achievers, persons who are doing well financially, but may have been upwardly mobile, who very often are in professional occupations, and who frequently are the visible "community leaders". The lower-middle class (III) are "working people", but doing relatively well financially, typically within white collar (clerical) occupations. The upper-lower class (IV) are "poor but honest" workers, persons working in factories, and often immigrants. The lower-lower class (V) approximate those whom Marx termed the "lumpenproletariat", in that they are perceived as the "people who scrape the bottom", persons on welfare. (Warner, 1949: 66-67.) Whatever the distinction, it is the case that no so-called class is homogenous in characteristics, or itself free of some additional hierarchical gradation.

Class distinctions are perceived by people on the basis of many indicators, the most fundamental of which is money — that is, inherited and earned wealth. The indicators that can and have been used by particular researchers in order to identify class composition are various, and can be used to various degrees of precision. The more gross the distinctions we wish to make, the easier time we have of it. For example, we could dichotomize and distinguish only the extremes of wealth and poverty. The distinction between the two classes could be in terms of possessions, such as money and negotiable securities, land, or housing. We would still have to decide arbitrarily what extent of possessions distinguish the superior to the inferior stratum, and where the cut-off points would be, but we could make the distinctions and be rather straightforward about it. But we would be lumping together persons who in many ways are distinguishable. A theoretically more meaningful dichotomization, one to which we will at times resort in the following chapters, would be to distinguish those who own productive property from those who lack such property and work for wages or salaries, or even are unemployed. That this dichotomization obscures considerable differences within each stratum is all too apparent, and for most sociologists, such a dichotomization would be of little utility. But it does summarize a fundamental difference between capitalists or those who control means of production, and employees, those who are dependent upon owners for their livelihood.

If finer distinctions are required, the task is complicated. Not only do we have the matter of arbitrary cutting points, but also the limited visibility of indicators. In feudal societies, symbols of wealth such as clothing or housing were highly distinctive by strata and very visible. But in modern Canada, short of the extremes, people dress approximately alike or drive automobiles approximately alike, even wear clothing and drive automobiles for which they have inadequate income. Quite obviously there remain distinctions in the quality and cost of clothing, automobiles, or housing, as well as other consumer items, and in the ease with which different persons may acquire them. The difficulty is in systematically identifying and distinguishing them, or in determining those few which would serve to be indicative of the others. In modern Canada, one such indicator, for example, might be housing, given the extent to which the single dwelling unit has become a scarce commodity. The notion that certain key items are indicative of one's class membership has resulted in a number of research procedures designed to measure social class.

F. Stuart Chapin developed four indexes of class, one of which he came to favour as most effective: the "living-room scale". (Chapin, 1928; 1933; Guttman, 1942.) Chapin found that evaluation of living room items was an effective representation of all possessions and of social status, in that the living room was the centre of family interaction and display. He evaluated the material and the "cultural" status of the items and their condition — matters such as presence, quantity, and nature of books and magazines, for example. To take an improvised example from Chapin's notion, one would expect different magazines in an upper-middle class home as opposed to a lower-class home, such as *Saturday Night* as opposed to *Readers' Digest*; or shelves of books containing titles such as *Culture Shock* as opposed to either the utter absence of books, or paperback titles such as *The Love Machine*. Or to consider furniture, the upper-middle class home is not likely to have a television set in the living room, where a lower-class home would. The differences in possession, as illustrated in reading materials, is not a matter of invidious comparison, but a recognition that different kinds of possessions and their uses do correlate highly with incomes, suggesting that they are effective methods of measurement.

In his community studies, Warner developed two principle methods of identifying classes; he called them Evaluated Participation (E.P.) and the Index of Status Characteristics (I.S.C.). He found the results from each to be highly correlated. (Warner, 1949.) They were first used in his famous Yankee City Studies (1941). The E.P. depends on the ratings or perceptions of a representative sample of members of the community. It is an attempt to specify the nature of the over-all "social-class configuration" of a community, as well as to specify the participation or life style of individuals within that configuration; the research depends upon the consensus on "matched agreement" of the respondents. (Warner, 1949: 47-71.) The I.S.C. uses four visible socio-economic items: occupation, source of income, house type, and dwelling area (Warner, 1949: 41) as indicators of class membership. The occupational dimensions distinguished independent businessmen, size of business, professionals, clerks, skilled, semi-skilled, and unskilled workers. The income dimension distinguished inherited and earned wealth, profits, salaries, wages, and welfare. Houses were distinguished by size and condition, and location or neighbourhood by reputation, facilities, and condition. (Warner, 1949: 122-154.) These were all scaled.

Such measurement approaches are particularly useful if we are dealing with a relatively small community. But if we wish to identify not simply social class membership in Cornwall, Ontario, or Kamloops, B.C., but social class in Canada, we would face the prospect of evaluating the possessions of millions of individuals, or equally unrealistic, requiring a panel of informants knowledgeable about the class characteristics of the entire society. We could, of course, resort to some representative sample and survey some proportion of the total population, but this would be a relatively inefficient research procedure as against alternatives.

A means of coping with measurement, other than by sampling or participant observation, is to analyze existing statistics as collected by agencies, such as Statistics Canada. Included among such available data, for example, is a breakdown of population by factors such as occupation, education, income, or even housing. Taken very literally, and recognizing room for error, two factors, education and/or income, have generally been used to provide crude but useful indicators of stratification. Such information is especially useful if we are comparing Canada to other nations. Income distribution, or educational distribution, would allow gross comparison of stratification systems, such as in terms of mobility opportunities as evidenced by the proportion of the population at varying levels of educational achievement. We could even persist in arbitrarily identifying strata.

A related device that has been used in many nations, and seems to produce approximately the same results in all industrialized nations, Canada included, is some form of *occupational ranking scale*. This technique was pioneered in the United States, with the NORC (National Opinion Research Centre) scale (1947), which ranked occupations and suggested cutting points or categories of ranked occupations, which could be taken to correspond approximately to strata or classes. National samples of Americans were required to rank order occupations by prestige. These rankings, when aggregated, produced an occupational ranking scale that has proved quite reliable and stable over time. And it has correlated highly with similar scales in other industrialized societies, including Canada. (Svalastoga, 1965: 23-31; Blishen, 1958.) Simply as a classroom exercise, we have consistently found that Canadian university students in the late 1960s and early 1970s were readily able to rank Canadian occupations such that their scores correlated with the 1947 American NORC scores to a value above .90 (perfectly identical rating = 1.0).

In Canada Bernard Blishen has devised a scale comparable to the NORC, and one that correlates very highly with it. Instead of prestige scores derived from a sample of Canadians, Blishen integrates public data regarding the educational requirements and the incomes associated with identifiable occupations in Canada as reported by Statistics Canada. The occupations are thereby rank-ordered, and cutting points are specified that serve to distinguish seven strata of occupation, or seven classes. (Blishen, 1958.)

Measurement devices like this serve to identify real differences in Canadian society. They do not identify real classes, in the sense of integrated and conscious groups. But they do approximate such identification and permit a magnitude of analysis — national rather than local — that would not otherwise be possible. Blau and Duncan, Svalastoga, and most sociologists argue that in modern industrial society the three fundamental dimensions of stratification — prestige, power, and privilege — are all reflected in occupation. This suggests that occupations are the best indicators with which to work. (Blau and Duncan, 1967: 6-7; Svalastoga, 1965: 29.) It should be realized that this is by no means a unanimous view. Some sociologists have been very critical of an occupational emphasis in stratification studies, suggesting that it leads to an emphasis upon status groups and not the fundamental existence of economically based classes. Usually such critics insist that the basic distinction must be between owners of the means of production and non-owners. (Parkin, 1971: 18-23; Anderson, 1973: 16; 122-123.)

Much of the data we shall work at for Canada is dependent upon occupation as the indicator of stratification. It may not be the best indicator, but it is widely available, and it allows the researcher to distinguish a very real non-propertied middle class. At times we shall distinguish specific occupations or sub-sets of occupations, following Canadian census distinctions. On other occasions, however, we will aggregate occupations, in the view that the fundamental distinctions are between the upper class of large property owners, controlling the means of production, and non-owners. Among non-owners we will distinguish the upper middle class, consisting of professionals, managers, and small businessmen; and the middle class proper of the sales, service and clerical occupations — the "white collar" group. The lower class or working class consists of skilled or unskilled workers, employed or unemployed. Farmers, an ambiguous occupational category insofar as stratification is concerned, we take to run the breadth of the industrial class spectrum, essentially sharing an affinity with the middle class and the lower class, depending upon the size and productivity of their holdings. They, along with small businessmen, control property, but on a modest scale; the Marxist concept of *petite bourgeoisie* seems reasonably appropriate, excepting the small marginal or tenant farmer. As we shall see, it is the middle range farmer in Canada who historically has often been a source of social protest and change.

Class Consciousness

Social classes distinguished by indicators, prestige rankings, or simple occupation are not classes in the sense in which the concept was used by Karl Marx. Marx emphasized that the economically distinguishable strata must develop a group awareness or *class consciousness* that would realize itself in political action. It is undoubtedly the case that in Canada today there are lower class, middle class, and upper class persons who believe themselves to be so, and act in their personal and class interests, seeking to preserve or alter the existing distribution of wealth to their advantage. But entire classes do not act as interest groups or political actors. Nor do all members of such classes recognize their membership, a failure that Marx called *false consciousness*. Thus individuals often act contrary to their apparent class interests, such as the worker, perhaps even a labour-union member, voting for the Conservative candidate, what in England has been labelled the phenomenon of the "working class Tory". (McKenzie and Silver, 1966.)

The conception of class consciousness is premised upon the importance and probability of class action to realize class interests. Consciousness means not only some awareness of like situations, but also organized action to realize class-related objectives. We shall be considering the extent to which the Canadian social classes have demonstrated a class consciousness, in the sense of recognizing and acting as a commonality.

Minimal Inequality plus Maximal Opportunity

Thus far we have emphasized the pervasive existence of some form of hierarchical differentiation. However, as remarked earlier, there is nothing in our analysis that suggests as necessary, or in any way condones, the extremes of wealth and power existing today in Canada and every other nation of the world, including socialist and communist nations. If one worries over filling positions and motivating behaviour, as do Davis and Moore, one can utilize a system of honorific awards as well as one can a system of material rewards, although there would be difficulties in implementation. Eliminating gross economic disparities would still involve some hierarchical differentiation by prestige and power. Conceivably, given equal material rewards there still might be competition for more attractive activities or roles, those which are perceived to be more intrinsically satisfying. But even such differentiation could be moderated, as by rotating roles, as is done to a very limited degree today in the Republic of China.

If we must reconcile ourselves to some measure of vertical differentiation, we need not be reconciled to systems that deprive members of society of the means to existence, or existence of comparable quality to more prestigious or powerful members of society. The differences in wealth which in Canada today are translated into differences in life style, as represented by quantity and quality of foodstuffs, medical service, and various consumer and service benefits, need not persist. That is, quite simply, differentiation could be quite minimal, devoid of material differences, and characterized by non-institutionalized and non-inheritable differences in power and prestige. Thereby society would approximate the perfectly egalitarian society. We emphasize that this levelling up need not concede or endorse elaborate welfarism. Rather, as a statement of theoretical and desirable condition, as opposed to probable or politic condition, it is to suggest the possibility of a radically different form of social organization, consisting of shared resources, and variable role performance implemented through socialization and honorific reward.

Ostensibly nations dedicated to organizing in keeping with Marxist principles were seeking such a situation through elimination of material or economic differentiation, although no communist nation has achieved or persisted in doing so. They never, however, sought to moderate differences in power and prestige, at least for the leaders who needed authority in order to successfully consolidate the revolutions and enforce communist definitions of society. An imperfect and limited attempt to minimize all forms of differentiation in a national society is that of Maoist China, where disparities obviously persist. Yet the communal ownership and production, the uniformity of clothing, the inter-change of intellectual and manual tasks, are intended to approximate a broadly based egalitarianism.

The point is that there is no evidence suggesting that stratification must take any specific form, nor that the differences among people must be gross, especially in material possessions. Thus, in Canada, whatever its political unlikelihood, we may conceive of a society of virtually equal economic distribution. The extent of differentiation, therefore, may be minimized, in theory, if not historical precedent.

Nor need it be the case that the generational institutionalization of any differences need persist. That is, such differences among persons as do occur need not be perpetuated across generations, as they now are in all nations, including communist nations.

Societies such as Canada's are characterized not only by marked and rather extreme stratification, but also by *inequality of opportunity*. Not only do some people have more things than others, they also have greater opportunity to acquire additional material items, not because of biological advantage or superiority, but because of social legacy. As opposed to other societies, such as traditional agrarian societies generally, in Canada, as in the industrialized nations of Europe and in the United States, we emphasize *achievement* over *ascription*. Quite literally, people are to receive what they earn. But quite obviously we have not eliminated people's ability to receive material advantage directly through inheritance, nor their inheriting greater opportunity.

Putting it conversely, there is considerable inheritance of disadvantage in Canada. There are social obstacles to success. Rather than equality of opportunity, the children of persons of higher status are more likely to themselves realize high status than are the children of low-status parents. Opportunities for social mobility do exist in Canada; but the probability of mobility of a middle-class child to a higher income or occupation, and in particular a middle-class male, is greater than that of a lower-class child. This is so even if other things are equal, which they are not, such as the influence of region in Canada, and the ethnic group membership or origin of Canadians.

Variation in mobility opportunity will be considered throughout this book. For example, we will consider unequal access to education. The point we wish to establish here is that we must be aware not only of the existence of inequality of wealth, power, or prestige, but also of inequality of opportunity to alter the status one has from birth. Lower-class children are less likely ever to achieve middle-class status, let alone upper-class status. Or, to take the not unimportant converse, children of high-status individuals are unlikely to be downwardly mobile, to occupy a social rank subordinate to that of their parents.

The very concept of social stratification includes the notion of rigidity or persistence; the system of differentiation in possession and advantage passes on from generation to generation through the family. But there is a theoretical alternative, one that is supposed to exist in practice in Canada and other western societies. Inequality of reward would co-exist with full and equal competition, such that the most worthy are the most rewarded. There would be inequality of condition, but equality of opportunity, as opposed to the inequality of condition and of opportunity that characterizes stratified societies. (Gilbert and McRoberts, 1975.)

In such a society, the inter-generational transmission of class membership and its advantages would be eliminated. People might receive greater rewards than others, but these would not be passed on to heirs. It must be stressed, however, that to dedicate oneself to equality of opportunity is different from dedicating oneself to equality of condition. Full equality of opportunity would still permit a system of considerably unequal rewards; it would be a *meritocracy* of reward dependent upon performance, with the competition renewed in each generation. It is a view, therefore, which concedes hierarchical differentiation, but rejects the necessary inheritance of that differentiation. Equality of condition goes a stage further, including equal competition for benefits, but insisting that differential benefits may be minimal, and will exclude unequal material reward. (Gilbert and McRoberts, 1975.)

This argument, it should be noted, is premised upon the view that the bulk of differentiation in modern societies cannot be attributed to genetic or biological differences, as some argue, but to social conditions. Undoubtedly some biological variations do affect human performance and differentiation, and these would persist. Thereby probably some inheritance or generational continuity in social status insofar as related to biologically vested skills or personal attributes will also persist in any social future. Unless that also, to continue our utopian speculation, were altered by some program of fully controlled breeding in order to homogenize biological inheritance. The obvious irony of this last suggestion is that in its very nature it is a challenge to idealist conceptions of human freedom and dignity. But, some such biological inheritance noted, we emphasize that inequality of condition and of opportunity are socially based, and thereby subject to social alteration. It is from this awareness that we may go on to consider some of the specifics of social stratification in Canada.

Conclusions

Social stratification consists of inherited and hierarchical distinctions among people in a society. Persons who share an approximately common social position, as distinguished principally by wealth, but also by power and prestige, are in our society thought of as belonging to a social class. Such classes are not legally and clearly demarcated, but there are several approximate means of identifying them, especially by concentrating upon occupation.

Class societies offer greater mobility opportunities than do closed societies, such as the caste or estate stratification systems of agrarian societies. But such greater opportunities are far short of equal competition for benefits. Rather, unequal benefits are accumulated and passed on through the family to succeeding generations in the form of wealth or learned skills. Thereby the relative class composition is maintained.

The inequalities that characterize a stratification system are not inevitable. Even if some such hierarchical differentiation is inevitable, the extent of disparity, especially economic disparity, may be extensively moderated. Certainly the institutionalized inequality that characterizes Canadian society as we will describe it in the following chapters is remediable, theoretically if not politically.

2

THE STRUCTURE OF INEQUALITY

The Myth of Classlessness

In Canada, as in the United States, we have tended to subscribe to the myth of a classless or a middle-class society. (Porter, 1965: 3.) What this means is that middle-class Canadians tell researchers that they perceive themselves to live in a homogeneous middle-class society. We are taught to think in such a fashion by our parents, peers, the media, and the schools. Additionally, we are taught that we succeed or fail by our own efforts. For middle-class persons this is a notion readily accepted. The school system is such that middle-class students are more apt to succeed academically and go on to satisfactory occupations and incomes and then continue to associate with other healthy consuming middle-class people. Thereby the myth of the middle-class society of equal opportunity is perpetuated. As one author sums it up, "Canadians see their society as 'classless' because the vast majority of persons with whom they interact are, just as they themselves are, members of the middle class. It is precisely because we perceive our structure in this way, that we ignore *both* the extremes, that is, poor and the rich. The larger the middle class, the less visible the extremes." (Hofley, 1971: 104.)

The middle class insulate themselves from extremes of wealth and poverty. Our working experiences and our residential communities are remarkably homogeneous, such that we only associate with people like ourselves. Paupers and millionaires are merely the stuff of television drama, and thereby unreal. The peculiar life-styles of power and wealth, or helplessness and impoverishment, do not intrude upon the daily lives of most Canadians. As we travel from home to work and back, to shopping centres, movie theatres, we do so in our private capsules along routes that never penetrate the slums or the exclusive communities of a city. And, as we Canadians for the most part do live in cities, we never really see, let alone experience, rural poverty. As Hofley notes:

> We have placed our Indians on reservations, effectively hiding them from the comfortable majority. Small rural farms, the majority of which are poor, look quaint on a Sunday afternoon drive. Regions of Canada such as the Atlantic Provinces, Western and Northern Quebec, Northern Ontario, many parts of the West (particularly the northern fringes), and the Northwest

24

Territories and the Yukon are seldom seen by the affluent except through uncritical tourist eyes. In some Canadian cities suburban commuters may drive through urban slums, but they certainly do not experience them in any meaningful way. (In most Canadian cities, one can drive around or over the slums and then avoid seeing them, except from on high). (Hofley, 1971; 105.)

Thus, it is important to be aware that although sociologists are capable of distinguishing strata in Canada, conveniently designated as classes, and although these classes do represent, as we shall discuss, very real and significant differences in style of life, class is to some extent a subjective matter as well as an objective economic condition. In the absence of a full awareness of the existence and the consequences of class distinctions in Canada, class-related inequalities are tolerated and persist, to the terrible disadvantage of many Canadians.

Nationalism and Classlessness

Another factor contributing to a moderation of class awareness is national pride and ideology. It is a well-worn feature of human collectivities that internal cleavages are obscured and a solidarity achieved by indulging in an opposition to some other group. This extends from the trivial to the sinister, from national flags and national hockey teams to national armies and foreign conflicts. We generally are socialized to accept an unquestioning allegiance to a nation and its decision makers, though in the Canadian experience, this socialization has had a regional as much as a national viability.

In these early years of Canada's second century, nationalism has moved well beyond the slogans and sentiments of 19th century "no truck or trade with the Yankees". The nationalist surge has a considerable significance and validity, although it may serve to deter genuine structural changes in Canada. Concern over Canadian ownership, control, and utilization of industry and natural resources or the composition of Canadian universities are matters fundamental to the nation; yet, perhaps to the detriment of dealing with the question of what kind of nation and at what cost.

Unfortunately, too, much of the nationalist pomp is mere window-dressing, akin to the "opiate" that Marx scornfully perceived religion to be. Elaborate circuses and games, such as Expo 67 or the Summer Olympics, or nationalist pop culture and pride in the latest "hit" by the Stampeders or the Guess Who, may contribute to the national awareness. But they will also divert serious confrontation of fundamental "human" issues within Canadian society, pre-eminently those relating to inequality.

The Marxist analyst would unhesitatingly suggest, with reason, that the Canadian "ruling class" is deliberately manipulating agencies of socialization, such as the schools and the mass media, in order to consolidate its position of class advantage. Thus the federal government licenses, scrutinizes, and subsidizes the broadcast media, and similarly shapes publishing, with the support of nationalists deploring the "American" influence. The national "publicly owned" television and radio network is explicitly intended to create and serve a national solidarity.

For example, indicative of this effort to generate a positive Canadian concept or identity was the Canadian Broadcasting Corporation's 1973 production of Berton's *The National Dream*. Such television efforts at making Canadian history "interesting" are fashioned after the heroic genre, a nation of grand vistas, men, and deeds. A hallmark of such programs is that they romanticize and emphasize anything that may be seen to contribute to a sense of Canadian nationhood. Such media myth making homogenizes serious political deficiencies and conflicts to the basic denominator of nation building. An illustration from *The National Dream* is the celebrated notion that the Canadian Pacific Railroad earned its keep from the outset, for it "saved the nation" by transporting troops to the West to put down Louis Riel and his rebels. The point to be taken is the assumption of the interests of Upper Canada as legitimate, as against the distinctive interests of another region of British North America. The actions of the Indian and Métis populations are said to be invalid in that they contradicted the ideological and economic interests of British-Ontario mercantilists in the precariously established new nation. In the light of expansion into the Northwest, in competition with the Americans, Canada's "first war" was a colonial war, not a mere police action against disloyal subjects; yet such an interpretation is not in keeping with national pop mythology.

In a time when we proudly wear Canadian flags on the seats of our American-subsidiary-produced Levis, we are celebrating in a superficial way a middle-class attitude of "all is right". Nationalism is both a euphoria and a scapegoating, insofar as it directs our attentions from internal problems and inadequacies to chauvinistic self-deception and indulgence.

There is a genuine dilemma, for to aspire to change Canadian society, as we do, requires that Canadians control their own society. To that extent, concerns such as those relating to the control and content of media of socialization, and of the Canadian economy, are legitimate. But Janus-like, such nationalism may retard realization of a satisfactory society.

Nationalism, including economic nationalism, is likely to involve a "liberation" of national wealth to the advantage of Canadians already disproportionately privileged, and it allows and promotes the persisting existence of underprivileged and welfare-maintained dependents, under the mantle of national pride and classlessness.

Micro-stratification

Class distinctions exist in Canada, and despite the insistence of classlessness, affect people's lives and intrude upon their awareness. There is some tendency to think of stratification exclusively in terms of large strata or classes characterizing a society. We are led to do so by Marxist theory, and generally by a total societal orientation, as in this volume, in which we are attempting to describe Canadian society. Such social classes will occupy us through much of our discussion, but we must also note the import of more local stratification, obtruding upon the day-to-day living of Canadians.

From early community studies, we know that people make fine distinctions among themselves. For example, as we previously noted, persons whom we would characterize as lower class will distinguish those who are unemployed or "shiftless" and those who labour to make ends meet, "poor but honest". (Warner and Lunt, 1941 and 1942; Lynd and Lynd, 1929 and 1937.) In a Toronto working-class neighbourhood it was found that the respectable employed were distinguished from those who "go wrong", who were viewed as "welfare bums". (Lorimer and Philips, 1971: 110-111.) Similarly, middle-class persons distinguish clerical workers from the self-employed and professionals, while upper-class persons are aware of the "*nouveau riche*" and "old money". (Warner and Lunt, 1941 and 1942; Lynd and Lynd, 1937.)

Not only does this illustrate that there are finer distinctions than those we conventionally associate with class, it notes that visibility of distinctions varies with one's social position. The lower-class person who distinguishes among members of his community in considerable detail is at the same time unaware of the distinctions among the middle and upper classes; they all live well and have money. The converse is also true. The upper-class individual will tend to lump together those of "inferior" social status. (Warner and Lunt, 1941 and 1942.)

Social distinctions noted only on a national level may obscure the salient features of the experiences of Canadians. For example, a region of Quebec may be characterized by low income levels and educational achievement on the part of its inhabitants, and we may thereby locate it in the societal wide stratification system. It tells us something about the life-styles and the opportunities for mobility of persons living in such a location. But at the same time it overlooks the finer awareness of the inhabitants themselves, which influences their behaviour, with whom they interact, date, and marry, for example.

The day-to-day meanings and distinctions in social status were described by Everett Hughes. In a Quebec parish he found, as researchers have found consistently, that businessmen and professionals of the town were the leaders. But in addition, status differences were indicated in ways other than by occupation. For example, owning or renting a pew in church was a sign of "stable position", and generally the professionals, businessmen, and local farmers did so, where labourers and the employees of town businesses did not. (Hughes, 1943: 95.) Similarly, attending high mass was indicative of higher and more stable social status. (Hughes, 1953: 97.)

In a study conducted in the inter-lake region of Manitoba, people engaged in the fishing industry were found to have a well-demarcated sense of local stratification. (Siemens and Forcese, 1963; Forcese, 1964.) Not only were the fishermen able to designate leaders with a high degree of consensus, what the uncharitable person might call the over-all pecking order became apparent. Generally, fishermen acknowledged as superior those among their fellows who were better educated and earned more money. These persons tended to be of Icelandic ethnic descent, and over all the Icelanders enjoyed higher status than fishermen of other ethnic origins. At the bottom of the local stratification hierarchy were the Indians. These "class" perceptions in turn influenced interaction more broadly, in terms of contacts among family members, exchanges of social visits, and mutual aid.

Another illustration of what we call micro-stratification may be taken from a study of "Jasper", as John Bennett called a region of southwestern Saskatchewan that he studied. (Bennett, 1969.) Bennett declines to argue that the 7,360 people of this area had a well-defined class structure; yet criteria of hierarchical differentiation were apparent. In the area lived ranchers, farmers, Hutterites, and Indians. The ranchers as a group had the greatest prestige, at the opposite extreme were the Indians, who were caste-like "non-people". (Bennett, 1969: 66; 74.) Even among the ranchers distinctions were apparent, as between the "town ranchers", "hill ranchers", "bench ranchers", and "sandhill and shortgrass ranchers". (Bennett, 1969: 66-68.) As a group, the ranchers were of British-Canadian and American origins; although their holdings varied in size and productivity, they maintained close kin ties. Similarly the farmers were distinguished according to their holdings; "prairie farms" were the rural middle-class prosperous farms, often British-Canadian owned. (Bennett, 1969: 68-69.) Generally persons of large holdings constituted an élite-like group in the region; the ranchers dominated town politics, along with local merchants and professionals, and the farmers dominated "agrarian politics", extending to provincial and federal levels. (Bennett, 1969: 183.) In addition to these distinctions, prestige was differentially assigned according to people's perceived worth, reminiscent of the prestige awarded the skilled hunter in hunting and gathering societies. Those who were seen to be efficient operators, and frugal, sober, co-operative, friendly, and the like, were held in high regard. Bennett thus speaks of "social credit", in the sense that such persons had credit or earned prestige. (Bennett, 1969: 184; 219.)

Such local or micro-distinctions are very salient to people's everyday behaviour and are usually more meaningful than the broader class differences in society as a whole, which are less visible to individuals. But in addition, local distinctions do reflect larger societal patterns; the example of single-industry towns in Canada is illustrative.

Community Stratification: Single Industry Towns

A characteristic Canadian community is the small town existing around a single industry, such as a mine, paper mill, or railroad. Such towns differ from those scattered about the country which grew up as local service centres or early foci of settlement. In these "old" communities are high proportions of impoverished Canadians, particularly in the Atlantic region. But single-enterprise towns are not impoverished; they enjoy a precarious prosperity. They are primary or extractive industry towns, and unlike the value-added industries of urban centres, exist so long as there is a profitable volume of extraction. As long as the mine or the forest holds up, or the company does not need to retool for continued resource exploitation, there may be a "good living" for the Canadians employed as workers in these towns, and for those few merchants and professionals who serve them.

In Canada there are several hundred single-enterprise communities, more than two hundred of them in the North beyond the agricultural zone. (Siemens, 1973.) For recent immigrants or for migrants from other parts of Canada, especially from rural Quebec and more recently from the Maritimes, such towns have represented opportunity. For example, recently Manitoba reported a recruiting program designed to bring labour to Manitoba mining towns, such as Thompson, offering wages far higher than those normally available in rural or urban areas.

Historically the single-enterprise town has been the creation of a principal employer. Such company towns depended utterly upon the company, and the company ran things. In the town the employees depended on the company not only for wages, but also shelter, services, and transportation to and from the isolated location of the town. The workers were recruited and imported by the company, and not linked by any prior organization or union. Looking specifically at northern Ontario and Quebec, Clark remarks that much of the labour force was drawn from rural Quebec, and argues that such migrants made possible the maintenance of union-free industry. Not only was the company in control, but in addition the Roman Catholic Church lined up in opposition to unionization. (Clark, 1971: 72.)

Because the towns are the creation of the employer and the planner, Lucas describes them as communities without tradition, and "towns of technology". (Lucas, 1971: 20.) Residents of such Canadian towns today tend to be young, married, of rural background, having no more than high-school level education, and from ethnically diverse backgrounds. (Jackson and Poushinsky, 1971: 32-40.) They are thus approximately lower to lower-middle class in origins. They also tend to be very mobile geographically. In one study, a sample of the residents of Fort McMurray, Alberta (pop. approx. 6000) more than half of the respondents (125 people) had moved five or more times, from town to town, "good job" to job. (Mathiasson, 1971.) Generally, such towns have provided economic opportunities for young, poorly educated Canadians, offering them relatively high-paying jobs, where in the South they might lack a job altogether.

These towns seem today to be characterized by good services or facilities, although complaints are characteristic and participation in community organization slight. (Wichern, 1972: v.) The high degree of geographical mobility, the physical isolation of the towns, and their newness all act to inhibit any sense of community and community action. But in addition, until recently these towns have been formally fully under the control of company administrators or provincial government administration. Not until the 1960s was there a clear pattern of local self-government, usually at citizen demand rather than at the initiative of the company or government administrators. (Wichern, 1972: iv-v.) Lucas suggests stages of town development; the "mature community" has succeeded from company government to local civic government. (Lucas, 1971: 91.) When we do find communities of long-standing self-government, the leadership of the community is vested in relatively few individuals.

When Michels offered his "iron law of oligarchy", he had been dealing with political party organization; but quite consistently sociologists have found similarly that a minority of individuals or an élite conduct effective decision making in towns and cities. Their leaders are characteristically the proprietors of businesses and professional persons. A town familiar to anyone who has travelled the C.N.R. mainline through Saskatchewan is Biggar: "New York is big, but this is Biggar". In 1960 Richard Laskin found that Biggar's adult population of about 1600 generated 5100 memberships in 36 varied voluntary associations. These associations required 666 officers, but only about 100 individuals at most provided leadership, and these people were either involved in the town businesses or were professional men. (Laskin, 1969: 20-22.)

Thus, the small town provides a stratification system in microcosm. The small-town businessman, lawyer, or doctor, ultimately subordinate to or dependent upon the corporate owners and managers, probably do not rank very highly in terms of status in Canadian society as a whole, especially relative to the national élite, which we shall describe. But within their communities they are of top rank, because of their influence with other townspeople.

The ethnic stratification of these towns is also a reflection of the larger society. The company officers, and the professionals, tend to be Anglo-Canadians, and the workers French Canadian or European immigrants. In Railtown, where the railway provided the sole industry, Lucas noted persons of British background in top-level positions, including those mechanically skilled among the workers. The rank-and-file labourers were French-Canadian, Polish, Ukrainian, Italian, and Indian. (Lucas, 1971: 30.)

Relating to their place in the over-all picture of stratification in Canada, the remarkable feature of these towns is their dependency and precariousness. If a Marxist had wished to create a prototype of capitalist-worker relations, he could have done little better than to devise such communities. They offer a situation wherein there is a virtual class polarization in the sense that there is no substantial middle class of clerical and service employees, or even many small merchants or professionals — although the small latter group is, as we have noted, of influence. In recent history the standard of services provided the labour forces of these communities seems to have been respectable, and the workers have earned incomes perhaps not otherwise possible. But they do so at the discretion of the company. Even when the company does not formally govern the town, they still own it, often literally, as in the ownership of the houses and other buildings. If the company closes down, the town closes down, and the workers are obliged to move on.

However, in the "mature" community, moving on is not so easy. Aging with the town, the work force becomes less mobile, in part because their skills may be obsolescent, but also because, as Lucas notes, they have an investment in homes. (Lucas, 1971: 91.) Letting the town die leaves the workers without employment, and without a home or the money invested in the home.

Thus, when Canadian International Paper decided to close down their mill in Timiscaming, Quebec, after 50 years of operation, the community of 2400 built around the industry seemed effectively to be closed down. In this instance, because they were not mobile, the workers fought to keep the mill alive. As the National Film Board titled their film on the affair, it was "The Town that Wouldn't Die". With government direct investment and support of a new corporate investor, plus the workers themselves purchasing shares in the mill, it has thus far continued operation. The town residents fought for their lives — including the local merchants who were particularly active in leading the opposition to the mill's closing, consistent with findings elsewhere stressing the leadership role of the small-town middle class or petite bourgeoisie.

These towns, therefore, are the creatures of interests external to them. Companies centred in urban areas, often outside Canada, control them, so that they are in a sense artificial communities of persons of subordinate class status, irrespective of whether or not the residents are conscious of, or find immediately salient, their subordination. They are typically communities of Canadians who in the larger society are of lower class status.

Urbanism

Another aspect of the Canadian pattern of privilege is the existence of dominant urban centres. In particular, for Canada as a whole, Toronto and Montreal have been pre-eminent. Within regions, other urban centres have had considerable influence, as Winnipeg in the prairies, especially early in this century. Vancouver on the west coast, and increasingly Edmonton in Alberta and through the Canadian northwest have also acted as major centres of wealth and influence.

About one-half of the Canadian population live in cities of 100 000 or more. Cities generally, and especially major centres, are the loci of finance, production, transportation and communications, services, education, and cultural activities. Starkly indicative of economic influence is the degree to which raw material is transformed into usable products in cities. Thus, Kerr notes, "Montreal and Toronto account for about 37 per cent of all 'value added' in manufacturing in Canada. These two cities have more employees in manufacturing than the four western provinces combined, and over twice those of the Atlantic provinces." (Kerr, 1968: 227.) If one extends the concept of city boundaries to include a 50-mile radius of Toronto and Montreal, we find concentrated over two-thirds of the manufacturing activity in Canada. (Kerr, 1968: 227.) Additionally, Toronto and Montreal house over 75 per cent of the leading nationally active corporation head offices, and 85 per cent of major financial institutions. (Kerr, 1968: 227.) It is because of this concentration of industrial activity, and the resulting prosperous life style, that Montreal and Toronto must be viewed as affecting the lives of every Canadian, increasingly so with increased communication and transportation efficiency.

Moving out from these two major metropolitan areas, we find other cities whose influence is characterized by specialized economic dominance. Thus in the West, Vancouver is characterized by forest products industries, utilities, and pipeline industries; Calgary and Edmonton by oil and gas industries; and Winnipeg — at one time expected to develop a status comparable to that of Toronto and Montreal — grain distributing and general merchandising, retail and wholesale industries. (Kerr, 1968: 242.)

That these activities are reflected in the lives of Canadians and the pattern of distribution of wealth is illustrated in income tax figures, where the greatest proportion of the total income tax paid in Canada is from Toronto and Montreal. (Kerr, 1968: 230.) Wealth, power, and prestige are concentrated in the cities, especially in those with major industrial and financial institutions. But the advantages are by no means homogeneously distributed.

Downtown and the Suburbs

Within the broad framework of overall affluence, within the cities there is a clear and enduring distribution of persons by social class through the metropolitan area. Investigation consistently points to a marked degree of ethnic and economic stratification. As in the United States, the inner Canadian city tends to be the locus of lower-status persons engaged in unskilled or semi-skilled occupations. Immigrant populations locate in the older inner areas of the city, succeeding to homes that have housed earlier waves of immigrants. In such areas, for example, are to be found the immigrant populations of Italian or Portuguese descent in the city of Toronto, the destination of the overwhelming majority of immigrants to Canada.

In addition, one may find in cities old British-Canadian neighbourhoods that have persisted in their ethnic identity and are working class in composition. Historically, Cabbagetown in Toronto has been such a case. Lorimer and Phillips described a Toronto example, the neighbourhood of Minster Lane, east of the Ontario-Parliament district. In 1961 the average family income in Minster Lane was $4025, as compared to the over-all metropolitan Toronto average family income of $5831. (Lorimer and Phillips, 1971: 8.) The residents were long-time home-owners in the neighbourhood, about half of them owning their houses. But they were relatively poor, working class, and of British origin. The men who were employed, half of them earning less than $3000, worked at such jobs as truck driving, warehousing labour, baking, and carpentering. Those who did work were the "respected" members of the community. (Lorimer and Phillips, 1971: 7-8; 35.)

In contrast to the downtown areas of Canadian cities, the suburbs are made up of middle-class professionals, often from Anglo-Canadian backgrounds. Thus the upper-middle class suburb of Crestwood Heights, with its doctors, lawyers, and managers, is oriented to occupational success. (Seeley, Sims, and Loosley, 1956.) Clark found that the majority of people moving into Toronto suburbs after the war were Canadian-born, of British origins, Protestant, and viewed themselves as "middle-class". (Clark, 1966: 98-99.) Clark notes also that from about 1961 there was some decline in WASP dominance, with some Jews and successful non-Anglo immigrant families moving into suburban communities. (Clark, 1966: 99.) Undoubtedly the non-WASPs were in quest of what might have been viewed as a better standard of life with respect to quality of housing, even at the cost of giving up the community and ethnic ties that would have characterized their inner-city lives. Yet additionally, as Clark concludes, they were people aspiring to an improvement in social status by seeking association with middle-class people already established in the suburbs. (Clark, 1966: 103-104.)

Even with such ethnic infiltration of the suburbs, they have tended to remain "pure". That is, certain suburbs are perceived to be, and are, largely upper-middle class and Anglo-Canadian, and often explicitly defined as exclusive. Rockliffe Village in Ottawa, Wellington Crescent in Winnipeg, or Westmount in Montreal have been stark examples of élite residential communities within urban centres. Similarly, Clark concluded that Toronto suburbs such as Etobicoke, Don Mills, Scarborough, and particularly "exclusive" suburbs such as Thorncrest Village, remained Anglo-Canadian bastions. (Clark, 1966: 100 and 212.)

The extent to which similar stratification by suburbs is true of other Canadian cities is less well documented, but in all probability much the same. It is not remarkable to suggest that in Canadian cities, as in the United States, there has been a middle-class exodus to the suburbs. Where the cities are characterized by growth through immigration, the old downtown area becomes the setting of the "new" non-Anglo ethnic groups, such as has been true of the "North End" of Winnipeg. The middle-class suburbs are characterized by, and perceived to have, specific ethnic identities, usually Anglo-Canadian, such as the suburb of St. James in Winnipeg, or at times Jewish, as Tuxedo in Winnipeg.

There is thus reason to state that residential segregation in Canada is as much by ethnic background as it is by socio-economic status, recognizing that in Canada the two factors are so intimately related. It has in fact been suggested that ethnic background is more important than socio-economic status (social class) in Canadian patterns of residential segregation. (Darroch and Marston, 1971.) Yet, over time, as successive waves of immigrants are assimilated in the sense of achieving some economic success in Canadian society, we may expect to find some continued breakdown in the segregation of suburbs, much as Clark described for Toronto, as some immigrant families or the second generation of these families move into predominantly Anglo-Canadian suburbs. This limited movement to the suburbs may be observed in Ottawa, for example, with some Italian-Canadian families moving from city-centre to the newer suburbs. But the present urban subcommunities or suburbs characteristically have been and remain the centres of Anglo-Canadian upper- and middle-class Canadians. And the prosperity enjoyed by these Canadians has not been characteristic of all regions.

Regional Inequality

Canada is generally conceded to be among a minority of the nations of the world, in that it is considered a developed or industrialized nation. Some analysts would dispute this by pointing up the high proportion of national income generated by extractive as opposed to manufacturing industries, or the high degree of foreign ownership. But it is nonetheless the case that by most indicators of development, such as average per capita income, per capita energy consumption, or standard of living, Canada belongs to an élite group.

Such indicators suggest an affluent society. Yet it is a misleading suggestion, for the considerable affluence that does exist obscures the disparate concentrations of affluence and poverty in Canada. Poverty among the aboriginal populations of the North and western provinces is not visible in such a simple figure. Nor is the welfare existence of populations in rural areas of the Maritimes, or in the slums of our large metropolitan centres. Relative to size, the greatest proportion of impoverished Canadians are to be found in rural locations and small villages of between 1000 to 10 000 residents. As a proportion of regional populations, the greatest incidence of poverty occurs in the Maritime provinces, followed by Quebec, the Prairies, British Columbia, and decidedly last of all, in Ontario. (Podoluk, 1968: 187-201.) Conversely, looking at the distribution of high status occupations, Blishen pointed out that of the 1961 male labour force, the greatest proportional representations of high-status occupations in the regions were in Ontario, the West, Quebec, and far last, the Maritimes. As we shall emphasize repeatedly in subsequent discussion, Canadian society consists of a regional stratification — that is, a hierarchy of privilege that distinctly clusters by region.

There are collectivities or strata based on social status that extend across the regions of Canada, such that one may still speak of nationwide classes. But the regional economic character obtrudes, as does the local stratification we have previously noted.

Any given occupation will be differentially evaluated and rewarded in different regions. For example, a medical doctor will have approximately the same social status in St. Johns, or Brandon, or Montreal, if we take the occupation and its educational and income correlates as a measure. But it is only an approximation. The income of a surgeon in a large urban centre will be greater than that of the general practitioner in Trout Lake. Similarly, within the small town the doctor may assume an almost god-like importance and prestige, where in an urban centre a doctor is one of many doctors and other high-status professionals. Yet, among his peers, themselves largely urban doctors, success and ability are taken to mean a specialized practice in an urban community, and thereby will be associated with greater prestige. Or to take another extreme, the labourer working for the city of Toronto will earn more than the labourer working for the city of Saskatoon; the work is the same, but the remuneration varies. Occupational scales such as we previously described aggregate by occupation and obscure their regional and local variations.

Trader Trudeau

Montreal Gazette

More important than variations in occupational worth, the opportunities for social mobility vary from region to region. Mobility opportunities are far greater in the large urban areas than in the smaller cities of Canada, or the rural areas. Indeed, opportunities for employment are greater. This has long been understood by Canadians who leave rural and small-town homes in order to make it in the big city, especially the big eastern cities. Little wonder, then, that we take for granted the phenomenon of "going down the road".

This is all somewhat obvious. Each of us has a notion of where we are apt to get a job or to earn more money. But however obvious, there is an important point to be made. Although most Canadians if asked would say that they were "middle class", and although we can estimate a class breakdown in Canada by occupation, there are nonetheless important differences in life-style and mobility opportunity from region to region. In that sense, there are several regional stratification systems: one for the Maritimes, another for Quebec, another for urban Ontario, another for the Ontario hinterland, for the Prairie provinces of Manitoba and Saskatchewan, for Alberta, or for British Columbia.

Regional disparity exists not because the federal government recognizes it, but because it has evolved with Canadian development. In a sense, the Canadian West and North have served as the colonies of the industrialized East, as "westerners" have argued. Historically high tariff and rail freight rates have profited eastern Canadian manufacturing industries and permitted the extraction resources of the West to be processed in central Canada, then resold at high cost in processed form. Although today the western provinces are experiencing apparent prosperity, vested in resource industries, the perception of "colonial" status persists. The insistence by non-industrialized provinces, such as Alberta, that they and not the federal government control their natural resources is an aspect of this regional stratification.

An indicator of disparities summarized by region is to be had in looking at "amenities" by region (Table 2-1). Thus, although considerable improvement is to be noted over 15 years, the incidence of such simple items as piped running water, exclusive use of bath, shower, and flush toilets vary markedly. Consistently and overwhelmingly the Atlantic provinces and the Prairies are least well served. Ontario, Quebec, and British Columbia are best supplied, although the Quebec figure is qualified by noting that, although piped running water is present to a greater degree than any other region, the exclusive use of a bath or shower is less common than it is in British Columbia or in Ontario.

Table 2-1

Occupied dwellings lacking selected amenities, by region

	Canada	Atlantic Provinces	Quebec	Ontario	Prairie Provinces	British Columbia
	percentage of all occupied dwellings					
Piped running water:[1]						
1956	18.2	34.2	5.0	11.5	46.3	5.7
1966	5.5	14.6	1.0	2.4	16.2	2.3
1971	2.7	9.6	0.3	1.1	8.0	1.3
Exclusive use of bath or shower:						
1956	30.5	56.4	26.9	18.9	51.8	12.4
1966	11.5.	31.7	10.5	5.4	20.0	4.3
1971	7.4	27.1	5.8	3.6	12.3	3.3
Exclusive use of flush toilet:						
1956	26.9	50.0	11.1	18.2	58.0	14.2
1966	7.5	25.0	1.8	4.6	21.6	3.9
1971	4.6	17.5	0.6	2.4	12.0	2.2

[1] Means piped running water inside the dwelling.

Perspective Canada, page 215, Table 10:13.
(Reproduced by permission of Information Canada.)

Generally, if we consider federal government granting as an indicator of regional status, three kinds of regions are distinguished: high incentive regions, moderate incentive regions, and low incentive regions. These approximate the incidence of economic deprivation. The regions are synopsized in the map, Figure 2-1.

Note that the Maritimes constitute the high incentive area, indicating greatest economic deprivation. Incentive region B encompasses the rural regions of Quebec, Ontario, Manitoba, Saskatchewan, and to a lesser degree Alberta and B.C. Incentive region C includes only the rural, small-town areas along the lower St. Lawrence from Drummondville, Quebec, to Renfrew, Ontario. Additionally, some special areas, towns or small cities in the Maritimes, Quebec and the prairie provinces — all major underdeveloped regions — are singled out.

The obvious point is that, of the populated regions, only the west coast, southern Ontario, much of Alberta, and some of Saskatchewan are excluded, apparently comprising prosperous Canada.

We can see the pattern more clearly if we examine regional variations

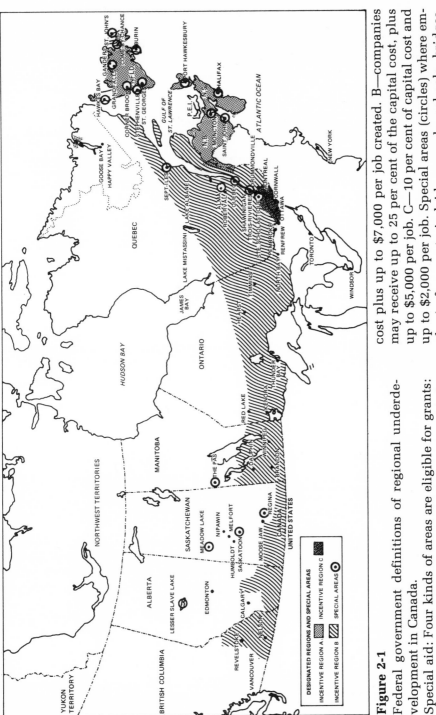

Figure 2-1

Federal government definitions of regional underdevelopment in Canada.

Special aid: Four kinds of areas are eligible for grants: A—where the highest grants go. Companies establishing there may receive up to 35 per cent of the capital cost plus up to $7,000 per job created. B—companies may receive up to 25 per cent of the capital cost, plus up to $5,000 per job. C—10 per cent of capital cost and up to $2,000 per job. Special areas (circles) where emphasis for grants is laid on roads, schools, bridges, sewers and similar municipal undertakings.

in the proportion of Canadians employed in industrially related activities, such as manufacturing, wholesaling, and finance. Overwhelmingly, southern Ontario and Quebec (the urbanized areas) outstrip all other regions of Canada (Table 2-2).

Table 2-2

Industrially related employment in regions of Canada, 1961

	% employed in manufacturing	% in wholesaling	% in finance
Southern Ontario and Quebec	73.0	54.5	66.0
Atlantic and eastern Quebec	6.5	9.0	6.0
Quebec and the Ontario Shield (except northern Ontario)	4.0	3.0	3.0
Northwest Ontario, Western Canada, and the North	16.5	33.5	25.0

Source: Kerr, 1968: 232

The extractive or primary industries and employment, with characteristically lower incomes, are distributed across the rest of the country, the hinterland of a small area of central Canada.

Another perspective on regional disparity may be gained from a perusal of rates of unemployment.

Figure 2-2

Unemployment Rates by Region

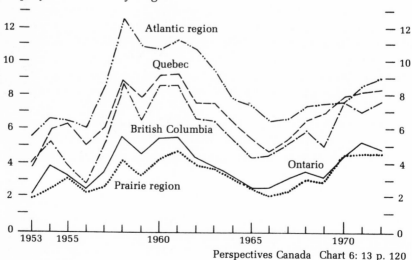

Perspectives Canada   Chart 6: 13 p. 120

The Maritimes manifest the highest rate of unemployment, followed by Quebec. Next is British Columbia, but unlike the Atlantic region, Quebec, or the Prairies, there is considerable migration to British Columbia, thereby magnifying the unemployment figure and to some degree shifting unemployment from other regions, such as the Prairies, to British Columbia. Thus, in some part, the Prairie region's favourable rate of unemployment reflects out-migration, while Ontario's favourable rate while experiencing in-migration reflects its industrialized prosperity. Generally it has been in those regions where the work force is engaged in primary rather than in industrial activities that out-migration has been highest in recent Canadian history, while Ontario, British Columbia, and most recently Alberta have been acquiring population from other regions of Canada and from other nations. (Stone, 1969: 9-11.)

Through these several indicators, it is noteworthy that the Maritimes consistently appear the least privileged.

Ethnic Stratification

Charter Groups

In addition to regional and urban differentiation related to stratification, we have been alluding to the fact that one's position in Canadian society is influenced by ethnic background. In 1965 the most important book in Canadian sociology appeared, John Porter's *The Vertical Mosaic* (1965). The title succinctly summarized the principle thesis of the work, that there is a clear and persistent relationship in Canada between social class and ethnic group of origin.

This was perhaps not a startling or surprising statement, for the honest observer of Canadian society would have long since noted this relationship. John Porter himself had published several papers on the theme over the previous twenty years. But although not new, the thoroughness of the analysis was new. And like many things people think they know, ethnic stratification in Canada not only had to be stated, but proven.

Porter wrote of the two "charter groups" who historically have comprised the nation — persons of Anglo-Saxon or British ethnic origins, and those of French origins. Each was party to the founding of the Canadian federal state, each constituted in a sense, a nation (1965). Yet, the one group was a conqueror, the other a conquered people. The nation, in a sense, was founded in a tradition of conquest and the related definition of superiority and inferiority. As Rioux has argued, with the conquest the old French aristocracy plus the clergy united with the English to form a new ruling group or "aristocratic compact".

(Rioux, 1971: 18-20.) The influence of this alliance persists to the present, despite massive post-war changes — witness the slight French-Canadian representation in industry, except as workers.

Thus the participation of the two "charter groups" in Canadian society has never been equal. They occupied, as aggregates, different strata along the stratification hierarchy. To put it simply, those of British origin have tended in disproportionate numbers to occupy high social class positions, of high income, prestige, and power, while French Canadians have tended disproportionately to occupy lower-class social positions. Across the nation, persons of British origin earn approximately 10 per cent more than the national average. This is true of all the provinces separately, except for Newfoundland (where the labour force is virtually of British origin, at 94 per cent), and Quebec, where those of British origin enjoy a startling level of income superiority, 40 per cent above the provincial average. Consistently, in all provinces, French Canadians earn less than the provincial income averages. (Canada, 1969: 17.)

The significant exceptions to the pattern of British-Canadian dominance and French-Canadian subordination have been in politics, the bureaucracy excepted, and in the control of the media. French Canadians have had access to high-status political positions, including, of course, that of Prime Minister of Canada. Moreover, they have occupied the positions of formal political power within the province of Quebec. In addition, ownership of the major Francophone newspapers has been French-Canadian. Also the French in Quebec dominate farming and have sizable representation in the retail trade and the construction industry. But in all other sectors of the economy they are in a minority ownership position within the province, and of course, in the nation as a whole. (Hall, 1973.)

Generally it has been the case that control of commercial or economic interests has rested with those of British origins. Thus, for example, the large chartered banks have been controlled by Canadians of British origin, as have Canadian industries. For example, to illustrate this feature of our society, consider Canada's two largest metropolitan centres, Montreal and Toronto. In Montreal, when we move beyond the political leadership which is French Canadian, and examine the economic "élite", we find disproportionate Anglo-Saxon representation. Where British participation in the Montreal labour force, including many professionals, has been declining, the Anglo-Saxon dominance at the top in major commercial organizations persists. (Rennie, 1953.)

Similarly in Toronto, the Scots and English have dominated high status, and additionally Kelner argues that the Irish now also have "entrance group status", since at least 1931. (Kelner, 1969.) Richmond had reported a few non-Anglo-Saxon corporate leaders in Toronto (Richmond, 1967: 70) and signs of multi-ethnic professions: similarly,

Kelner (1969: 32) had reported greater access by non-Anglo-Saxons. But she concluded that the "core" élite was still "pure", while the lower or "strategic élites" where non-Anglo-Saxon ethnic groups were gaining access were not accepted by the "core-élite", did not significantly interact with the "core-élite", and were less influential. (Kelner, 1969: 232.)

Mosaic

In contrast with elite composition, still looking at Toronto, we find large numbers of Italian and Portuguese immigrants or descendants. After the British, persons of Italian descent make up the largest ethnic group in Toronto, with more than 250 000 people, the majority of whom are first generation. (Jansen, 1971: 207.) They tend to be employed as labourers, and generally are encouraged to come to Canada for unskilled and semi-skilled jobs. (Jansen, 1971: 212-213.) This is quite unlike persons recruited in the United Kingdom and western Europe, favoured locations for professional recruitment and high-status entry to Canada.

National figures show that the labour force is clearly stratified by Canada's several ethnic groups. For example, Table 2-3 indicates occupational categories in Canada by ethnic background. High-status occupations such as the medical and the administrative or managerial are occupied by persons from the British Isles, or those who are Jewish, in greater proportion than other ethnic groups. The exception is the high proportion of Asiatics in medicine. Thus, relatively, the other ethnic groups are distributed in greater proportion in lower status occupations, from labour to white collar. Service occupations and labour sectors such as farming, forestry, logging, and mining are heavily represented by the French, Italian, Polish, and native Indian populations.

There are other data illustrative of the ethnic nature of the Canadian economy and society. For example, Briant looked at the construction industry and found its four components dominated by different ethnic groups. (P. Briant, cited in Hall, 1973: 90.)

> The control and operation of large industrial engineering equipment is almost entirely in the hands of the Anglo-Saxon group in the country. The financing of construction is in the hands of this group and the Jewish group. Small scale contracting has become very much a special field for French-Canadians who employ Italians in substantial numbers. The organization of real-estate has fallen very largely into Jewish hands — they predominate heavily among the real-estate businesses. . . .(52)

Generally, even in the province of Quebec, French Canadians are strongly represented in only a few sections of the economy. As Hall notes, commenting on data reported by the Royal Commission on Bilingualism and Biculturalism, French Canadians own 90 per cent of

Table 2-3

Ethnic group by occupational group, 1971

	British Isles	French	German	Hun-garian	Italian	Jewish	Nether-lands
				per cent			
Managerial, administrative and related	5.2	3.7	3.6	2.8	1.8	10.7	3.5
Natural sciences, engineering and mathematics	3.1	1.8	2.7	4.7	1.3	2.6	3.3
Social sciences and related	1.0	0.9	0.6	0.6	0.3	3.3	0.7
Religion	0.3	0.4	0.3	0.2	0.1	0.2	0.4
Teaching and related	4.3	4.5	3.6	3.1	1.6	5.2	3.2
Medicine and related	4.1	3.6	3.5	3.4	1.1	4.9	3.6
Art, literature, performing arts and related	1.0	0.9	0.7	1.3	0.6	2.1	0.8
Clerical and related	18.5	14.7	13.4	11.5	9.7	18.8	11.9
Sales	10.4	8.7	8.7	6.7	6.7	24.2	8.8
Service	10.6	11.2	10.6	11.9	13.0	4.9	10.6
Farming, horticulture and animal-husbandry	5.4	4.4	12.5	9.4	1.8	0.4	14.2
Fishing, hunting, trapping and related	0.4	0.2	0.1	- -	- -	- -	0.2
Forestry and logging	0.6	1.3	0.5	0.4	0.2	- -	0.4
Mining, quarrying including oil and gas field	0.6	0.9	0.7	0.7	0.4	- -	0.4
Processing	3.1	4.9	3.7	4.2	6.2	1.4	3.8
Machining	2.4	2.8	3.4	5.8	5.2	0.6	3.1
Production, fabrication, assembly and repair	5.9	8.2	7.6	9.7	15.6	6.4	6.9
Construction trades	5.6	6.9	7.9	7.2	15.3	1.7	8.1
Transport equipment operation	4.2	4.5	3.5	2.5	2.6	1.7	3.5
Material handling and related	2.4	2.2	2.3	2.4	3.4	0.8	2.3
Other crafts and equipment operation	1.4	1.3	1.1	1.0	0.7	0.6	1.1
Not stated and not elsewhere classified	9.5	12.0	9.0	10.5	12.4	9.5	9.2
TOTALS	100.0	100.0	100.0	100.0	100.0	100.0	100.0

Table 2-3

Ethnic group by occupational group, 1971 – Concluded

	Polish	Russian	Scandi-navian	Ukrai-nian	Asiatic	Native Indian	Other	Total
	per cent							
Managerial, administrative and related	2.8	3.0	3.8	2.9	3.1	1.5	2.6	4.3
Natural sciences, engineering and mathematics	3.2	3.1	3.0	2.5	7.1	1.1	3.3	2.7
Social sciences and related	0.6	0.6	0.7	0.6	1.0	1.3	0.7	0.9
Religion	0.1	0.2	0.2	0.1	0.1	0.1	0.1	0.3
Teaching and related	3.0	3.5	4.0	3.5	4.7	1.6	3.0	4.1
Medicine and related	3.2	3.2	3.7	3.0	8.5	2.2	3.8	3.8
Art, literature, performing arts and related	0.7	1.1	0.8	0.7	0.9	1.1	1.0	0.9
Clerical and related	14.2	13.7	13.7	14.8	14.7	6.9	12.2	15.9
Sales	7.2	7.7	9.1	8.4	9.1	2.7	6.3	9.5
Service	13.1	11.6	10.7	12.9	16.9	12.4	15.7	11.2
Farming, horticulture and animal-husbandry	8.0	10.4	12.6	11.6	2.2	5.9	5.0	5.9
Fishing, hunting, trapping and related	--	0.1	0.5	0.1	0.3	2.6	0.2	0.3
Forestry and logging	0.5	1.0	1.2	0.4	0.2	6.2	0.6	0.8
Mining, quarrying including oil and gas field	1.1	0.8	1.1	0.9	0.2	1.0	0.7	0.7
Processing	4.8	4.6	3.0	3.8	3.9	4.1	4.6	3.9
Machining	4.1	2.7	2.0	2.7	2.2	2.2	4.4	2.8
Production, fabrication, assembly and repair	8.9	6.4	5.2	6.9	8.0	4.4	11.0	7.4
Construction trades	6.7	7.4	8.0	6.5	2.0	9.8	7.4	6.5
Transport equipment operation	2.8	3.9	4.0	3.7	1.4	3.6	2.5	3.9
Material handling and related	2.9	3.0	2.6	2.8	2.0	3.1	2.5	2.4
Other crafts and equipment operation	1.0	1.1	1.2	1.1	0.8	0.7	1.0	1.3
Not stated and not elsewhere classified	11.1	10.9	8.9	10.1	10.7	25.5	11.4	10.5
TOTALS	100.0	100.0	100.0	100.0	100.0	100.0	100.0	100.0

Source: Perspective Canada, Table 13: 24: pp. 279-280. Reprinted by permission of Information Canada.

farms, 60 per cent of retail trades, and 50 per cent of construction ventures. (Hall, 1973.) In all other fields in Quebec, French-Canadian ownership is a definite minority. For example, in the wholesale trade French-Canadian ownership is 40 per cent, in transportation and communication 40 per cent, in manufacturing 25 per cent, and in mining 20 per cent. (Hall, 1973: 53.)

A last example may be taken from career patterns in the federal civil service. Recently much publicity has been given to Trudeau government policies emphasizing bilingualism in the civil service, and supposedly favouring French Canadians in hiring and promotion. Yet Beattie and Spencer found that where objective factors such as education were important, as they are supposed to be in a modern bureaucracy, ethno-linguistic background affected careers, and did so to the detriment of Francophones, who were less apt to realize high positions in the civil bureaucracy. (Beattie and Spencer, 1971: Beattie, 1975.) French Canadians are found to have lower starting salaries than their English-speaking counterparts, and lower rates of salary increase and promotion. Even at the same level of educational qualification, persons of French mother tongue have lower average annual incomes than do the English. (Canada, 1969: 214; 218.)

Given the varying positions of ethnic groups in the economic order in Canada, as indicated by occupations and income representation, it is an obvious corollary that persons of different ethnic backgrounds have different life-styles. That is, all Canadians, depending on ethnic qualifications, do not live the same way in terms of consumption of basic commodities, luxury items, or shelter. It is apparent, for example, to put it crudely, that if the stratification system is such in Canada as to favour certain groups, they are the persons who will dress better, eat better, and have better shelter. And the different ethnic groups will tend to be segregated by community, even within our cities. For example, we have already noted evidence that ethnic background is an important basis for residential segregation, particularly as it is related to income.

The English and the French charter groups, the one privileged and the other economically underdeveloped, have constituted the major and most visible components of the "vertical mosaic". As Canada attracted immigrants from other nations, other ethnic groups found niches in the Canadian stratification hierarchy. As successive waves of immigrant peoples reached Canada, they tended to be associated with distinguishable regions of Canada. Thus, added to the Scots of the Maritimes, the English of Ontario, and the French of Quebec, came German settlements in the Maritimes and Ontario, and middle-European populations such as the Ukrainians on the Canadian Prairies. And always at the bottom of the class order, the "non-people", the Indians and Métis.

The structure of privilege, weighted in favour of the English-speaking person of United Kingdom origin — the WASP, or white Anglo-Saxon Protestant — relegated the late-coming immigrant peoples to inferior occupations, and to the new less-populated frontier territories. Not only did such people, as individuals, face obstacles to mobility, from blatant prejudice to sheer unequal resources, they settled regions of the country that were often of marginal productivity, slipping out of the agricultural belt. Those who settled the arable land of the Prairies experienced wildly fluctuating prices for their crops. When mineral resources were added to grain as staple western products, the populations still filled the role of primary producers, and processing was confined to eastern Canada.

This in general has been the basis of a western-Canadian, ethnic-related perception of subordinate status and subsequent protest, as we shall consider in Chapters 4 and 5.

Current Immigration

Ethnic stratification is not just a matter of historical experience. We can distinguish a pattern of immigration in which certain ethnic groups enter the nation to fill low-status positions, others to occupy high-status positions. For example, British and American immigrants are more likely to be highly educated persons, with professional training, than are people from other nations. They are privileged and favoured immigrants, for "they are like us," and easily assimilated. Opportunities for emigration from such nations are good because of the posting of Canadian full-time immigration officers who are readily accessible, unlike the situation in, for example, Africa or Latin America. Not only are they advantaged relative to other immigrants, in Quebec and in the Maritime provinces, immigrants from the United Kingdom and the United States are more likely to fill high-status positions than are Canadian born. Rarely are United Kingdom immigrants of working class occupations. (Richmond, 1969.) On the other hand, Italian immigrants to Canada consistently assume unskilled tasks, and rarely do their members include professionals. Generally, professional credentials from nations other than the United States, England, or to some degree western Europe are not freely recognized by Canadian authorities, whether in government or in professional associations, thereby reinforcing this immigration pattern.

This point, that different ethnic groups enter the nation at different status levels, is illustrated by Bernard Blishen, who considers the extent to which various immigrant groups are under- or over-represented in higher status positions in Canada. The higher status positions are classes one to three of Blishen's occupational ranking scale. In the summary reproduced in Table 2-4 for the provinces of Ontario and

Quebec, all groups above the line in each of the three classes are over-represented; all those below the line, under-represented. The groups appear in order or degree of representation.

Table 2-4

Rank distinction of Canadian and foreign born (1946-1961) in Quebec and Ontario by degree of over- and under-representation in Classes 1-3

(above line over-rep.: below line under rep.)

	Class 1		Class 2		Class 3	
	Quebec	Ontario	Quebec	Ontario	Quebec	Ontario
1	U.K.	U.S.	U.S.	U.S.	U.S.	U.S.
2	U.S.	Asia	U.K.	U.K.	U.K.	U.K.
3	Scand.	U.K.	Scand.	Canadian	Scand.	Canadian
4	Asia	Canadian	Asia	Scand.	Hungary	Scand.
5	Hungary	Hungary	Oth. Europe	Asia	Asia	Asia
6	USSR	Scand.	Hungary	German	German	German
7	Polish	USSR	German	Oth. Europe	Polish	Hungary
8	Oth. Europe	Polish	USSR	USSR	Oth. Europe	USSR
9	German	Oth. Europe	Polish	Hungary	USSR	Oth. Europe
10	Canadian	German	Canadian	Polish	Canadian	Polish
11	Italian	Italian	Italian	Italian	Italian	Italian

Source: Blishen, 1970: 123. Table VI.

Reprinted from the *Canadian Review of Sociology and Anthropology*, Vol. 7:2 (1970) p. 123, by permission of the author and the publisher.

Note that the Italians are consistently the least equally represented for each of the three upper classes in each of the two provinces. The persons of American or British birth are the most over-represented for each class in each province. In Quebec, Canadians, which means French Canadians, are under-represented in each of the three higher classes.

The pattern of ethnic privilege is also clear on a region-by-region basis. In each region, and especially in the Maritimes and Quebec, persons of British or American background not only were better represented than immigrants of other ethnic groups, but they were also better represented than native-born Canadians in the top three classes. (Blishen 1970: 124.) And in each region, the percentage of British and American immigrants in the upper strata has increased since 1946. Conversely, in each region the ethnic group with the lowest representation was the Italian, while in both the Maritimes and in Quebec, Europeans generally were better represented in the upper strata than were Canadian-born. (Blishen, 1970: 124.)

Once an immigrant has arrived, ethnic background affects degree of success. Anthony Richmond found that the children of white-collar immigrants from the United Kingdom tended to be upwardly mobile in

Canada, while, conversely, the children of white-collar immigrants from Europe tended to fall in status relative to their fathers. (Richmond, 1964.)

The pattern of immigrant recruitment has reduced Canadian-born opportunities for high-status positions, and the pressures to train Canadian-born for such positions. Through Canadian history, as Porter demonstrated, professionals have tended to be imported (Porter, 1965: 54-56), usually from England and more recently from the United States. These are persons who are easily assimilated, for in language and custom they are similar to the dominant Anglophone charter group, and they have skills required in an industrialized nation. Canada has thereby been able to educate to the university level an extremely small proportion of its population.

The Ruling Class

The Economic Elite

The extent of inequality in Canada cannot be seen entirely in labour force statistics such as we have been using, for these exclude the enormity and the concentration of wealth and power. Thus, in addition to his analysis of ethnic stratification in Canada, a second major aspect of Porter's work consisted of an analysis of that minority of Canadians who held pre-eminent power in Canadian society, the counterparts of those whom C. Wright Mills had characterized in the United States as the "power élite". (Mills, 1959.) Porter analyzed the men of power in business, labour, politics, and federal bureaucracy, the mass media, universities, and religion. Ultimately, the structure of the economic élite was to attract more attention, perhaps inevitably, for the concentration of economic influence appeared of such magnitude as to shape the very character of Canadian society.

Porter concentrates upon Canadian-owned corporations in the bulk of the analysis. He suggested that 985 Canadian residents, holding directorships in 170 "dominant" corporations, banks, and insurance companies, constituted the economic élite. (1965: 234-263.) This would mean, putting aside non-Canadian ownership for the moment, that 985 individuals dominate the economic life of Canadian society, and hence, dominate and control Canada. He finds a family continuity in the social background of these people, suggesting that the élite is virtually closed; or to put it differently, that the upper sector of the Canadian stratification system extends across generations. (Porter, 1965: 275.) Of those in this élite, 118 were trained in engineering or science and 108 in law. (275-277.) Generally, professionals and persons with financial backgrounds dominated the élite, numbering 607. (Porter, 1965: 380-381.) Members of the élite were not necessarily university trained. A group notably excepted from formal university training were heads of banks. (279.) In ethnic background, over 90 per cent were of British background; only 6.7 per cent of the 760 were French Canadian. (286.) In all 18 per cent of the élite group were estimated to have been of lower-class origins, while 37.8 per cent were of upper-class origins. (Porter, 1965: 390.)

In a recent investigation that follows up on Porter's work, Clement (1975) finds much the same situation. The élite remain Anglo-Canadian. Clement found much the same background in training as had Porter, with some increase in law backgrounds. He established that the élite had become more closed to entry, with 59.4 per cent of the élite from upper-class backgrounds, 34.8 per cent from middle-class backgrounds, and only 5.8 per cent from working-class backgrounds. (Clement, 1975: 172-223.)

In addition to Canadian economic power, there is the matter of non-Canadian control of corporations operating in Canada. Porter acknowledged the growing importance of non-Canadian corporations. Aside from the absentee decision making such ownership represents, it means that the profits of Canadian corporations are to a significant degree being acquired by non-Canadians, by Porter's estimate more than half the profits. (Porter, 1965: 269.)

As Clement points out, however, Porter's data related to a unique period of Canadian economic history. The period immediately after World War II, and especially 1948-50, where Porter's analysis concentrates, was one of industrial boom and relative independence in Canada. The British were out, and the Americans not yet in. (Clement, 1974: 52.) In his work, using up-dated information, Clement stresses the very marked increase in non-Canadian corporate make-up. He found that Canadians were active and in control of financial (banks and insurance companies) and utility corporations, but not in industry. (Clement, 1975.) Over all, in firms of $25 million in assets or more, Clement finds 62 per cent of the directors are outside of Canada, as contrasted to Porter's estimate of 27 per cent. (Clement, 1974: 25.)

Clement attributes this pattern to Canadian policies, including tariffs, and the mercantilist tradition in Canada which profited from American-based industrialization (1974), much as Teeple argues that traditional mercantilists and government policies encouraged American industry in Canada. (Teeple, 1972: 21.)

In general, the corporate power in Canada, both foreign and Canadian controlled, was viewed by Porter to influence government to a degree that their interests are protected by government, or as Porter more generously put it, the economic environment is "stabilized". (Porter, 1965: 270-271.) In light of such evidence, and theoretical views suggesting that "economic" power shapes a society, the economic concentration found by Porter and Clement indicates a well-defined ruling class. Many social scientists have stressed that economic power is the basis of political power, and that the economic elite or ruling class controls not only the economy but also government and the society. (Miliband, 1969; Anderson, 1973; Mills, 1959.) In discussing conflict and change in Chapter Five, we shall consider further the influence of economic interests.

Government and Bureaucratic Elite

Political decision making is also classbound. The class bias in political achievement has been clearly established through Canadian history. Ward demonstrated that M.P.s elected from 1867 to 1945 clearly tended to come from middle- and upper-class occupations. Law in particular has been a dominant occupation in political careers. (Ward, 1950.) In more recent analysis, Forcese and de Vries find that the class pattern has persisted, with 60.9 per cent of all candidates for Parliament in 1972 holding high-status occupations, while 75.7 per cent of those elected were upper status. (Forcese and de Vries, 1974.) Also, Presthus calculated five class levels on the basis of education and occupation, and estimated that 71 percent of M.P.s were from the upper two classes. (Presthus, 1973: 275.) Similarly, Richard van Loon found that cabinet ministers overwhelmingly were of professional backgrounds in the period from 1867 to 1965. (Cited in Manzer, 1974: 241.)

Given that those of Anglo-Canadian background have been over-represented in high-status occupations in Canada, it follows that Anglo-Canadian representation in politics has also been high. By formal structure, the system of political representation ensures that non-British Canadians will be represented, so that the ethnic concentration such as it exists in the economic sector has not developed, especially with regard to French-Canadian representation. Thus French Canadians have always been well represented in formal politics, including cabinet positions federally. But other ethnic groups who are numerically fewer than are French Canadians in Quebec do not do as well, because they tend to have lower access to the higher status occupations, such as law, which tend to be requisites for federal electoral success.

The ethnic pattern of privilege is clear when we go on to examine the composition of the bureaucratic élite in the federal public service. In the federal bureaucracy, the top positions of the deputy minister level are predominantly filled by Anglo-Canadians, despite publicized efforts to emphasize the employment of French Canadians. Other ethnic groups are "scarcely represented", except for Jews. (Porter, 1965: 442.) Beattie also found that the career success of federal employees at middle levels of employment was related to ethnic background, to the detriment of Francophones. (Beattie and Spencer, 1971; Beattie, 1975.)

In his work, Porter found that his bureaucratic élite of 202 persons were largely university educated (78.7 percent), and tended to be English Canadian, although the 13.4 per cent French Canadian were largely in top-rank positions. (Porter, 1965: 441-442.) In the public service generally, there is bound to be a pattern of upper-middle class persons occupying important bureaucratic positions. This would have to be as a matter of definition; operationalization of class usually involves education and income, while hiring practices of the meritocratic public service require educational qualification as a prerequisite of executive or career appointments. The ethnic bias enters in light of a pattern of ethnic selection or over-representation in achieving university-level education in Canada, favouring those already of high status and of British-Canadian origin, as we shall discuss in Chapter Three. Thus, in terms of class background, Porter calculated that, although only 18.1 per cent of the bureaucratic élite could be described as upper class, 68.7 per cent were of middle-class background. (Porter, 1965: 445-446.) Presthus similarly calculates that 97 per cent of the bureaucratic hierarchy consisted of persons of the upper three class levels in his framework, that is upper-through-middle-class background. (Presthus, 1973: 275.)

Because the bureaucratic élite is by definition dependent on educational attainment, it seems more open than the economic élite, with its persisting family affiliations. Yet to describe the bureaucracy as open would assume not only fully objective hiring practices, but also that the Canadian educational system had been producing adequate personnel; Porter notes that some bureaucrats, however, were educated abroad, usually in the United Kingdom. (Porter, 1965: 445.) Fundamentally, to speak of the bureaucracy as open would require one to assume that the educational system is equally accessible to all Canadians. In fact it is not, as we shall see in Chapter Three.

The Other Side

We may close our overview of the structure of stratification in Canada by recalling the polar extreme of the Canadian élite — that is, poverty in Canada. In the rural areas of the country, in the small towns, particularly the old small towns, and in the old inner city of slum housing, we find Canada's impoverished. In the rural areas, they reside in substandard residences, often engaged in subsistence farming or fishing or trapping. These are the families of the rural Maritimes, of rural Quebec and northern Ontario, and the West. They are often Indian and Métis people on reservations, where their communities constitute semi-colonial territories governed by provincial and federal bureaucrats; or increasingly, as in the inner city of Winnipeg, they are "welfare Indians".

Even disregarding the enormous wealth of some families in Canada, and subduing figures in national averages, the enormity of poverty in Canada is striking. In 1965 the Economic Council of Canada reported that 61.6 per cent of Canadian non-farm *families* earned $7942 or less. (Harp and Hofley, 1971: 17.) The average Canadian family income was calculated to be $6669, as contrasted to the top fifth of family incomes, the 38.4 per cent of Canadians earning an average of $13 016. (Harp and Hofley, 1971: 17.) We stress that this is family income, and not individual income. Table 5 summarizes the over-all Canadian non-farm family income.

Table 2-5

Distribution of non-farm family income before tax

| | Distribution of Total Income | | | Average Income per Family |
	1951	1961	1965	1965
Lowest income fifth of families	6.1	6.6	6.0	$ 2,263
second fifth	12.9	13.4	13.4	4,542
third fifth	17.4	18.2	18.0	6,102
fourth fifth	22.5	23.4	23.5	7,942
top fifth	41.1	38.4	38.4	13,016
all families	100.0	100.0	100.0	6,669

Source: "The Basis for Concern", selections from the 5th and 6th Annual Reviews of the Economic Council of Canada, 1968-69 in Harp and Hofley, 1971, p. 17.

Contrast such economic conditions to the suburban lives of professionals, and the basic inequities of Canadian life are starkly painted — the Maritime worker in a fish-processing plant, with his $6000 per year income, contrasted to the surgeon or the dentist, earning a national average of around $40 000. Thus, even excluding big business money, the extent of economic inequality in Canada is profound. What this means in terms of real lives rather than anonymous numbers is impossible to portray in words or in figures.

Using 1961 data, Podoluk operationally defined poverty on the basis of a study of 2000 randomly selected families. She found that the average Canadian family spent about half of its total income on subsistence items — that is, food, clothing, and shelter. On this basis, she suggested that a family spending 70 per cent or more of its income on such staples was at or below the poverty level. This measure indicated that more than 25 per cent of Canadians were impoverished. (Podoluk, 1968: 185.)

This is probably a modest conception of poverty. It allows little scope for non-subsistence spending: nor does it make allowances for families of more than four members; for families of four or more, the poverty income in the calculation by the 70 per cent criterion was still $4000. (Canada, 1971: 7.) Other more recent estimates of poverty show much the same population proportion at the poverty level. The Senate Committee on Poverty estimates for 1969 that about one in four Canadians was below the poverty line. (Canada, 1971: 12.) Single individuals were the category of Canadians showing the greatest percentage of poverty, followed by two-person and five-person families. (Canada, 1971: 11-12.) The Senate estimates, by family size, and specifying the Senate poverty line incomes, are summarized in Table 2-6.

Table 2-6

Poverty rates by family unit size, 1969

Family unit size	Senate Committee poverty line income	Poverty rate
	$	
1	2,140	38.7
2	3,570	28.4
3	4,290	16.8
4	5,000	15.6
6.2 (5 or above)	6,570	28.5

Source: *Canada, 1971: 12. Reprinted by permission of Information Canada.*

Most of the poor live in urban areas, for that is where most Canadians live. Relative to the size of the rural population, however, rural poverty is massive. About 21 per cent of the total population live in rural areas, but 45 per cent of Canadian poverty is in rural areas. (Canada, 1971: 18.)

Similarly, because their populations are larger, most of the poor live in Ontario and Quebec. But as a proportion of population, the highest incidence of poverty is in the Maritimes (Canada, 1971: 18), and it is higher among Francophones than Anglophones. (B & B III: 84.) The greatest degree of poverty found in any group is that experienced by the native peoples of Canada.

Indian and Eskimo peoples have lately, with some assistance from the federal government, been pressing economically significant land claims. But these publicized successes merely serve to underline the miserable existence of the bulk of the native peoples. The Indians, Eskimos, and the Métis, who even lack treaty rights, have been relegated to the lowest rung on the Canadian stratification hierarchy, one somewhat analogous to that of the outcastes or untouchables of Indian society. Their indigenous cultures were all but wiped out by Anglo-European territorial expansion and trading, and even today their northern lands are designated for hydroelectric developments such as the James Bay project in Quebec or the Churchill River Falls project in Manitoba. The Indian peoples have not been allowed to compete on their own terms or those accorded most Canadians. Illustrative of their status is an estimate of services: in 1966, 80 per cent of Indian homes lacked sewers, septic tanks, flush toilets, running water, or telephones (Boroway, 1971: 213), items that we in Canada think of, not as luxuries, but as bare necessities of ordinary living. In 1965 Boroway reports that Indian families received an annual average income of $2000 or less; 47 per cent of Indians received well below average at $1000 or less. (Boroway, 1971: 213.)

The greater tragedy of such poverty is that it is institutionalized; there is inequality of condition, but there is also inequality of opportunity. The prospect in contemporary Canada of a child from a lower-social-class family achieving social mobility to middle-class status is very slight, although that is precisely what is supposed to happen in Canada, largely through the universal system of education. The future of the educational system is the topic of our next chapter.

Conclusions

Canada is a nation of economic extremes. The pattern of relative advantage points clearly to regional, rural-urban, and ethnic disparities. Generally, the Maritime region seems least plugged into Canadian affluence, and Ontario metropolitan areas the most prosperous.

It seems clear that Canadians operate at two levels of consciousness. On the one hand, because the majority of Canadians live well and are insulated from extremes of wealth and poverty, there persists the notion that classes do not exist in Canada. Yet, in every-day lives, Canadians are acting in ways that acknowledge a class awareness, satisfied in the belief that such differences are not fixed and will be overcome in time through the upward mobility of individuals.

The basic structure of Canadian organization consists of class-related distinctions. In Canadian towns we find stark relations of control and dependency; in Canadian cities and regions, we find clear patterns of hegemony and economic superiority. And running through this structure is a persisting pattern of distinction by ethnic background, with Anglo-Canadians dominating Canadian business and bureaucracy, such that top levels of Canadian wealth and power seem ever more closed to non-charter group Canadians. Such chances as do exist for mobility are slight, and distributed differentially by rural-urban residence, region, and ethnic background. And where there is mobility, it is mobility into the middle class, and not the upper-class élite or ruling class.

3

SOCIAL CLASS AND OPPORTUNITY

The Myth of Equal Opportunity

The idea of a classless Canadian society has been, as we noted in Chapter Two, a persisting insistence of middle class Canadians. What this belief seems to express is the idea that such inequities as do exist in Canada are surmountable, and the reflection of personal ability and subsequent success, or failure. That is, the related mythology is that of equal opportunity to compete for unequal rewards, a situation realized in a genuine frontier situation or in the ideal meritocracy. It is not equality that is being celebrated, but fair competition to be unequal.

Although Canada shares the North American belief in the existence of such equal competition, the myth has perhaps been made more of in the United States than it has in Canada. The open American frontier, with settlement preceding government authority, contributed to the image of the United States as a fabled land of opportunity. In contrast, it has been argued that Canadians, never experiencing anything comparable to the American Revolution or the American "wild" West, have always been more tolerant than Americans of inequality, and less impressed with fables of mobility. (Lipset, 1963: 25.) In this vein, Gad Horowitz suggests that English Canada has always stressed a more conservative, less egalitarian orientation, one emphasizing "aristocratic responsibility". (Horowitz, 1960: 19-21.)

Consistent with these differing American and Canadian orientations, the school systems seem to have had different definitions and effects in the two North American nations. In the United States education was early defined as a means to mobility, to a degree perhaps less ambiguous than in Canada. But more than that, education in the United States included a political socialization stressing a definition of "Americanism" and American individual and national success. In Canada, education has been élitist, the pastime of the privileged. As Neatby argues, the American and Canadian school systems, superficially similar (except Quebec), operated from different philosophies; in the United States there was a notion of "progressive education" and "training for citizenship", while in Canada the orientation was not to the Canadian nation and success, so much as to the British Empire, and to continuity and tradition rather than to change. (Neatby, 1972: 12.)

Yet in Canada as in the United States, there has been the illusion of limitless potential for economic benefit, vested in vast lands and material resources available for exploitation. True, historically Canada tended not to be the first choice of immigrants, perhaps because it was perceived to be "too English". Through much of its history, Canada has been a stepping-stone to the United States, land of "success" for immigrants landing in Canada and for Canadian-born. In both nations, too, the myth of boundless riches was tarnished somewhat by the drastic poverty and disruptions of the Great Depression. (Neatby, 1972.) For many Canadians the memories of the 1930s linger on, with bitterness only somewhat moderated by nostalgia. But even these "dust bowl" days of the decade of the 1930s were viewed, in retrospect, as an aberration, rather greater in duration than originally prophesied, but only a temporary disruption of economic growth. Moreover, even in the depression, many North Americans were inclined to ascribe such poverty or non-success to the individual, although, as we shall see in Chapter Five, there was significant opposition to government policies. Certainly in "good times" the myth of equal opportunity, founded on an ethic of Protestant individualism in both Anglophone Canada and the United States, led to the blasé rationalization that if an individual was not successful, it was his own fault, and not that of any social conditions. Thus, French-Canadian poverty and meagre representation in business was ascribed to a flaw in individual character and collectively of the ethnic group rather than to the nature of Anglophone influence and power, the role of the Catholic Church, or of traditional Quebec educational institutions.

Perhaps in the current decade we are less inclined to ascribe success or failure exclusively to individual efforts. We begin to realize, for example, that unemployment and under-employment can also trap the highly educated. Yet, we still are inclined to be rather glib and proud in viewing the successes we achieve, although perhaps critical and cynical about the successes of others, such as those indulging in what has come to be called executive privileges and "rip-offs". When we view the unemployed we are still inclined to speak of the "lazy, shiftless" poor living on welfare. We encounter reports of Indian poverty, or perhaps stumble upon "undesirable" neighbourhoods, and oft as not will resort to the notion that Indians are "drunken, lazy, and just no good, or else they wouldn't live like that." In each such instance we respond to the superficialities of the situation, secure in our own relative prosperity, rather than evaluating the social conditions that bring about and support such individual behaviour, and often prevent any alternative. That is, we still evaluate an individual, and are inclined to attribute his status to pure achievement. Yet, in point of fact, Canadians tend to inherit the social-class status of their parents.

A key factor in the chain of social condition linking the social class of a family, opportunity of children, and social class of mature children is that of formal education.

Education and Mobility Opportunity

Expansion

The North American ethic of democratic equality is committed to universal literacy, and more recently, with greater affluence and technological expertise in society, to a notion of universal education to the extent of an individual's abilities. To some extent these notions are now shared in some form or another by all of the industrialized world.

The drive to maximal education tends not to be viewed in the classical sense of making a better rounded individual, as Cardinal Newman expressed in his famous essay *On Education*. Nor is it premised on the aristocratic concept of training an individual to better make use of his leisure time. Rather to some extent there has been the notion in the United States, and perhaps less clearly in Canada, of education for better citizenship. But even more dominant is the idea that the formal educational system is the principle mechanism of training people in the skills required by and for industrial/commercial expansion, and at the same time providing opportunities for social mobility in Canadian and American societies. Thus the 1950s and 1960s in the United States were characterized by massive government financial assistance to school systems, particularly with a view to servicing minority groups, such as urban blacks and Puerto Ricans.

In Canada, critics pointed up the élitist nature of Canadian education, insofar as Canada educated to the university level only a very small proportion of her population; in 1961 only approximately 8.5 per cent of the labour force had some post-high school education, and not necessarily a university degree. (Porter, 1967: 114.) Critics further noted that we produced very few persons with graduate degrees, and tended to import our professionals. (Porter, 1965.) But by this time the American definition of education as a development of human national resources, the key to continued economic development and prosperity, and a means of extending opportunity to all Canadians without any direct intervention in the distribution of wealth and privilege, had become the accepted panacea. The 1950s witnessed an incredible expansion of educational institutions in Canada, supported by all levels of government and ultimately all taxpayers, with the burden carried by urban taxpayers in rapidly growing cities. By government sector, the federal government increased its support for all levels of education between 1950 and 1970. But education is constitutionally the responsibility of the provinces, and the greatest cost and increase in spending were borne by provincial governments. Meanwhile, the proportion of total costs met by student fees decreased.

In addition to the new emphasis upon education as a good invest-

Figure 3-1

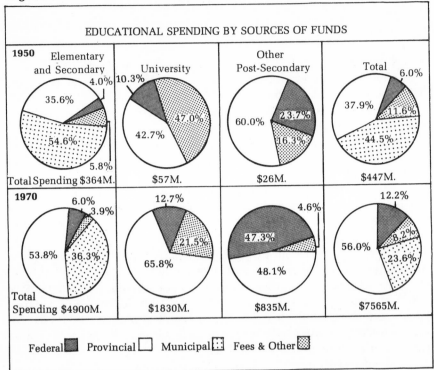

EDUCATIONAL SPENDING BY SOURCES OF FUNDS

1950 — Elementary and Secondary: Total Spending $364M. (4.0%, 35.6%, 54.6%, 5.8%)

University: $57M. (10.3%, 47.0%, 42.7%)

Other Post-Secondary: $26M. (60.0%, 23.7%, 16.3%)

Total: $447M. (6.0%, 37.9%, 11.6%, 44.5%)

1970 — Elementary and Secondary: Total Spending $4900M. (6.0%, 3.9%, 53.8%, 36.3%)

University: $1830M. (12.7%, 21.5%, 65.8%)

Other Post-Secondary: $835M. (4.6%, 47.3%, 48.1%)

Total: $7565M. (12.2%, 8.2%, 56.0%, 23.6%)

Federal ■ Provincial □ Municipal ⊡ Fees & Other ▨

ment, part of the expansion in educational institutions was simply demographic, for by the late 1950s the schools were dealing with the children of the post-war "baby boom". These were the children reaching the universities during the 1960s. Thus all levels of education, from primary through university, expanded drastically.

This created an enormous demand for physical plant. Particularly coupled with the rural to urban migration there was a burst of school building in city suburbs. At the same time, universities were building facilities and entire new universities were created, particularly in Ontario.

Necessarily, of course, in addition to buildings, qualified personnel were required. But because of the prior pattern of educating a very small percentage of Canadians to post-high-school levels, such trained personnel were not available. Thus school teachers and university professors have had to be imported, characteristically from the United Kingdom and the United States. Because of the prior underdevelopment of Canadian education, middle-class positions as educators now were being filled by non-Canadians. Over all, the competition for skilled educators, whether Canadian-born or immigrant, has worked to the advantage of wealthy urbanized central Canada, and to the disadvantage of rural regions, especially Quebec and the Maritimes. Thereby the

Figure 3-2
Growth of Enrolment Crests

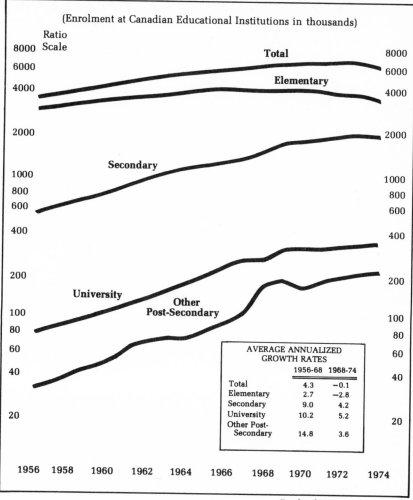

(Enrolment at Canadian Educational Institutions in thousands)

	AVERAGE ANNUALIZED GROWTH RATES	
	1956-68	1968-74
Total	4.3	−0.1
Elementary	2.7	−2.8
Secondary	9.0	4.2
University	10.2	5.2
Other Post-Secondary	14.8	3.6

Bank of Montreal Business
Review, Oct. 1974, p. 1.

socio-economic advantages of urban Ontario and other centres is reinforced insofar as the quality of education is concerned, as indicated by teacher qualifications and by the quality and quantity of the facilities provided. If "quality" education was the means to occupational success, then areas of Canada have been relatively deprived of such opportunity for occupational success. Nova Scotia excepted, the Maritime provinces are dramatically below all other areas of Canada in the proportion of teachers "fully qualified". In New Brunswick, as in Quebec (Roman Catholic schools), for 1962-63, fewer than 50 per cent of the elementary and secondary teachers were qualified, in the sense of junior matriculation plus two or more years of professional training for elementary teachers, and senior matriculation plus one or more years of training for secondary teachers. Newfoundland and Prince Edward Island had fewer than 25 per cent of their teachers so qualified! The highest proportions were found in Saskatchewan, Ontario, and British Columbia.

Table 3-1

Percentage of elementary and secondary teachers fully qualified, 1962-63.

Province	%
Newfoundland	21.2
Prince Edward Island	21.2
Nova Scotia	68.0
New Brunswick	37.9
Quebec, Roman Catholic	44.2
Quebec, Protestant	62.2
Ontario	85.3
Manitoba	77.3
Saskatchewan	86.6
Alberta	78.9
British Columbia	86.1

Source: Canada, 1969: 33. Reproduced by permission of Information Canada.

The Schools

The push to increased education did mean that educational attendance became more nearly universal. By 1961 universal school attendance of youths to age 15 was all but realized in Ontario; but in Quebec and the Maritimes, especially Prince Edward Island, this was least so.

Especially when one compares populations aged 15 attending school to populations aged 16 and 17 attending school, it is apparent that the regional variation in quality of education and existing privilege is operative. By age 17, the greatest proportion of continued school attendance is, in 1971, in Canada's most industrialized and urbanized province, Ontario. Once again, the lowest attendance proportions are

Table 3-2.

1 Elementary and secondary levels of public, private and federal schools.

2 Excluding Quebec for 1971.

NOTE: In relating enrolment figures to population data, percentages over 100% are shown, suggesting that there are more pupils in school than there are in the population. This anomaly occurs mainly because the data for pupils and the figures for population are derived from different sources, the former being school enrolment data and the latter Census of Canada figures.

Table 3-2

Percentage of the population aged 15 to 17 years attending school[1]

	1961		1966		1971	
	Male	**Female**	**Male**	**Female**	**Male**	**Female**
		per cent				
Newfoundland:						
15 years	95.2	96.1	87.2	89.4	93.0	92.0
16 years	72.9	64.6	78.4	71.6	75.6	73.6
17 years	39.7	30.4	46.9	35.7	45.9	40.1
Prince Edward Island:						
15 years	84.5	102.1	85.8	93.0	88.3	96.3
16 years	67.3	80.9	66.8	78.4	82.1	88.7
17 years	44.6	47.9	54.1	60.9	59.2	60.4
Nova Scotia:						
15 years	92.2	94.8	94.1	93.5	91.7	93.4
16 years	68.5	70.2	78.9	82.0	79.6	81.9
17 years	46.4	41.6	56.2	57.2	60.2	60.2
New Brunswick:						
15 years	88.9	89.5	89.5	90.6	92.2	92.7
16 years	62.2	63.7	74.9	78.6	82.9	82.9
17 years	48.7	42.7	58.2	57.3	63.4	58.2
Quebec:						
15 years	77.9	68.9	87.1	84.9	..	..
16 years	53.9	40.7	71.2	64.1	..	..
17 years	29.0	14.2	46.6	34.7	..	..
Ontario:						
15 years	90.8	90.7	99.3	99.1	99.5	98.2
16 years	75.9	75.3	90.5	89.1	91.3	89.8
17 years	61.8	54.7	72.6	65.3	79.8	73.8
Manitoba:						
15 years	94.3	95.0	97.9	96.8	94.3	96.7
16 years	75.2	74.6	88.2	86.4	88.2	89.2
17 years	59.2	46.8	67.3	60.5	66.7	63.3
Saskatchewan:						
15 years	92.1	97.3	97.5	97.5	94.0	95.7
16 years	79.5	80.6	88.2	88.4	85.8	87.6
17 years	61.5	57.6	68.6	64.5	63.4	60.4
Alberta:						
15 years	93.1	96.0	94.4	95.6	96.1	96.4
16 years	80.9	81.1	87.4	87.8	88.1	89.8
17 years	63.8	57.4	66.8	60.7	68.8	62.3
British Columbia:						
15 years	112.4	115.7	106.1	104.9	95.1	96.0
16 years	97.2	95.9	99.0	99.5	88.9	87.6
17 years	84.2	82.7	90.1	86.3	64.0	57.5
CANADA:[2]						
15 years	88.9	86.9	94.6	93.9	96.7	96.6
16 years	69.9	65.1	83.3	80.6	88.3	87.8
17 years	50.8	41.4	63.1	55.3	71.1	65.8

Source: *Perspective Canada page 70, Table 4.4. Reproduced by permission of Information Canada.*

found in the Maritimes and, relying upon 1966 figures, Quebec. Thus the "drop-out" phenomenon is concentrated in the least prosperous areas of Canada, reinforcing the existing pattern of unskilled labour and lower-class occupations.

Increasingly, following the American pattern, high-status occupations in Canada have come to require university-level education. Professional occupations have, of course, always demanded university degrees, but the requirement of university education as a qualification has extended to virtually all middle-class occupations. Table 3-2 shows that those most apt to finish high school, and thus able to go on to university, are found in Ontario.

The Universities

University enrolments swung up through the 1950s and 1960s as did educational enrolments generally. "Instant universities" were built, non-Canadian faculty recruited, and increasing enrolments were projected by university administrators into the indefinite future. However, by the first four years of the 1970s the enrolments have stabilized.

That more people than ever before in Canadian history are now going to universities is certainly a fact. Undergraduate university enrolments are estimated to have increased by 331 per cent from 1945-46 to 1964-65. (Porter, 1967: 115.) However, the fact has to be tempered. University enrolments may have increased, but there is reason to believe that the proportion of Canadians achieving university education is still far too small. If the United States is taken as a comparative

Table 3-3

Minimum years of educational attainment of male labour force, aged 25-34 and 55-64 Canada 1961 and United States 1960

Minimum Attainment	Per cent of male labour force			% by which U.S. exceeds Canada
	Age Group	Canada	U.S.A.	
8 years elementary school	25-34	81.5	88.9	9
	55-64	55.5	68.8	24
4 years high school	25-34	28.2	57.2	103
	55-64	16.9	26.1	52
University degree	25-34	6.0	14.7	145
	55-64	4.2	7.0	67

Source: *Economic Council of Canada*, cited in: Porter, 1965: 120.
Gordon W. Bertram, *The Contribution of Education to Economic Growth: Staff study No. 12*, Economic Council of Canada, Ottawa, Queen's Printer, 1966, Table 12. Reproduced by permission of Information Canada.

model, and if only the male labour force is considered, it is found that Canada is educating to the secondary and university level less than half as great a number as the United States, and the disparity is growing rather than decreasing as of 1961. (Porter, 1967: 120.) That is, the younger age group (25 to 34) is educated in higher proportions than the earlier generation (55 to 64), but the increase is far greater in the U.S.A.

Middle Class Education

However, it remains true that more Canadians are being educated than ever before, including an increasing proportion to the university level. By 1972 the proportion of the population 14 years and over who had completed a university degree had almost doubled.

Table 3-4

University attainment of population 14 years of age and over, 1960-1972

	Population	— University—	
	1,000's	Some	Complete
1960	11,699	3.8	3.1
1965	12,930	5.0	3.6
1966	13,305	5.7	4.0
1967	13,717	5.4	4.0
1969	14,470	6.9	4.8
1972	15,673	—	5.9

Source: *Perspective Canada*, Table 4.1, p. 69.
Reproduced by permission of Information Canada.

This has led some observers to conclude that mobility opportunities in Canada must therefore have been increasing. That is, since more education means better and higher status jobs, and since there were more people getting higher education, this must mean that more people were getting better jobs. This complacent interpretation overlooked two rather obvious features of the education explosion — an upgrade of job qualifications, and an increase in the number of middle-class females taking university degrees.

(1) Upgraded job qualifications

There has been a redefinition of job requirements; many positions requiring university-qualified personnel in the 1950s and 1960s were positions requiring high school credentials in the 1940s and earlier.

This is not to deny that with industrial growth some new skilled positions not previously part of the labour structure have come to be, requiring educated personnel. But what has also occurred is a general upgrading in the educational credentials required for positions even where such credentials had nothing to do with the task at hand. Therefore, by stratum there was less mobility than appeared to be the case. A head of a family would hold middle-class status, for example, by virtue of an executive position in some firm; yet that parent might well have only a grade nine education. However, that middle-class man's sons would now require, and probably obtain, a university degree to hold down the same kind of job and the same social-class status. There would have been an educational upgrading, but no inter-generational social mobility.

(2) *Female educational achievement*

In addition, from that middle-class family, not only would we be apt to find male children attending universities where their children did not, but also female children. Much of the influx into universities in Canada in the 1950s and 1960s was by females. Where before the war a girl was not usually expected by her parents to attend university, by the 1950s and 1960s female attendance was more and more taken for granted. Today, glancing about any classroom in any Canadian university, particularly in Faculties of Arts, you would find around 35 per cent of the class consisting of females, where prior to World War II the proportion would have been far less, around 20 per cent. Where in 1920-21, only 20.3 per cent of bachelors and first professional degrees were taken by women, in 1968-69 the proportion was 37.2 per cent. (Manzer, 1974: 202-203.) Considerable as the change has been, it should additionally be noted that female access to the professions has not increased to the same extent; in law, in 1921 only 3.7 per cent of the total number of graduates were women, and by 1961 the proportion was still only 5.2 per cent. Female careers in medicine have fared somewhat better compared to law; in 1921 4.4 per cent of the medical school graduates were women, and by 1961 the proportion was 7.9 per cent. (Calculated from data reported in Porter, 1964: 117.)

Professional schools aside, there has been a change in established role definitions that had previously relegated females to secretarial and nursing schools, if they received post-secondary education at all. This change shows up in statistics pointing up higher university enrolments. Now females from middle-class homes were competing to a greater degree with middle-class males.

There was, therefore, not as great a change in educational achievement by social class in Canadian society as statistics on university enrolment at first glance suggest, if the composition by gender is not distinguished. Middle-class young women were attending universities in greater numbers than they were in the 1940s, and in a sense inflating the statistics. That is, the increase in educational enrolments did not mean expanded opportunities for all classes. It was in considerable proportion middle-class females and not lower-class males who were accounting for the increase. Once educated, they have still been tending to enter the labour force in the traditional female professions, especially teaching and nursing, and other white-collar semi-clerical roles. (Manzer, 1974: 223-234; Gilbert and McRoberts, 1975.) Despite education and middle-class status with its correlated Anglo-ethnic origins, Canadian women entering the labour force still tend to be excluded from high-status jobs in the professions and the corporate and government bureaucracies (see Table 3-5).

Table 3-5

Percentage female labor force participation by selected occupational categories, 1901-1961*

	1901	1961
White collar	20.6	41.3
Professional	42.5	43.2
Clerical	22.1	61.5
Sales	10.4	36.7
Manufacturing	24.8	16.8
Transportation and communications	1.4	7.9
Service	68.6	57.1

*Source: Department of Labour, Manpower Trends in Canada (Ottawa: Queen's Printer, 1965). Reproduced by permission of Information Canada.

(Cited in Gilbert and McRoberts, 1975)

Undoubted mobility opportunities have existed in Canada, through the 20th century. But they were not as numerous as some interpretations would have it. Serious social barriers to mobility have persisted, and Canadians have not been proceeding equally through the educational system. The very institution that was meant to secure mobility has not equally influenced all social classes. A basic indication of this is the extent to which people aspire to and plan on higher educational levels, and higher occupational levels, than their parents. We shall see that aspirations as well as achievements are inherited by class.

Educational Aspirations and Class

Stratification is a structural feature of societies in the sense that it consists of distinguishable collectivities or groups of people dependent upon property or upon labour for their incomes, and these relations are perpetuated over generations. There are, of course, also attitudinal components of a stratification system. We know, for example, that persons from different social classes will tend to have different attitudes regarding sexual behaviour, aggression, cleanliness, promptness, to cite a few examples. So, too, they will have different attitudes and expectations regarding educational and occupational "success".

In Canada and in the United States there are numerous studies exploring the attitudes of young people to educational and occupational achievement. Indeed, few areas of sociological interest have generated as much empirical research. The assumption of researchers has been that young people's attitudes towards educational and occupational achievement influence actual behaviour and serve as indicators of actual behaviour. Thus the level of education to which a boy or girl aspires or expects to achieve, and the kind of job aspired to and expected, affect the extent of education and kind of job actually obtained.

But, of vital importance relative to the egalitarian myth, these aspirations are not randomly distributed in the population. Rather, stated aspirations are indicative of and correlated with social class.

Research in Canada has confirmed that aspirations are principally a function of the social class level of one's family, and rural versus urban residence — not altogether unrelated factors. (Siemens, 1965; Pike, 1970; Breton, 1972; Rocher, 1975.) Thus one is more likely to aspire to and expect to achieve a university degree if one comes from a middle or upper-class family as opposed to a lower-class family. Conversely, one is more likely to wish and expect to drop out of the educational system before completing high school, or immediately upon completion, if one comes from a lower-class family as opposed to a middle-class family. Reflecting educational aspirations, middle-class youth are more likely to aim for high-status occupations, such as medical doctor or lawyer. (Siemens, 1965; Pike, 1970; Gilbert and McRoberts, 1974.)

Even when I.Q. is controlled, the class bias persists. In a Manitoba survey of rural and suburban high school students, it was found that within each of the upper and middle classes, higher I.Q. students (male and female) tended to aspire to higher levels than did lower I.Q. students. But within the lower class, higher I.Q. was not related to higher aspirations; that is, high I.Q. lower-class students tended not to have aspirations higher than other lower-class students, nor aspirations as great as less "intelligent" middle- and upper-class students. What seemed to affect higher aspirations among lower-class students was teacher encouragement. (Forcese and Siemens, 1965: 23-24.)

Similarly, Gilbert and McRoberts report that in an Ontario sample of grade 12 students, lower-class male and female students in the university-prep or five-year stream in high school tend to plan other than university education, whether planning to enter the labour force or go on to some other form of post-secondary education. This is in contrast to the university-level aspirations of middle- and upper-class students of the same I.Q. range. (Gilbert and McRoberts, 1974: 13-14; 32-33.)

In a major study of 150 000 secondary school students from all provinces, Breton found that the high I.Q. lower-class student was less apt to want to go on to post-secondary education than the middle and upper class students of high I.Q.s. (Breton, 1972: 140.) Though the trend was somewhat less pronounced than in the findings of other researchers, Breton generally found that the educational plans and occupational aspirations of students related to social class, with a slighter proportion of lower-class children intending post-secondary education of any sort, and tending to aspire to lower-status occupations (Tables 3-6 and 3-7).

Table 3-6

Educational plans of boys and girls in sample, related to social class of father

	Finish High School		Attend Post-secondary	
	%	%	%	%
Father's Status				
High	86	88	73	69
Medium	81	83	66	61
Low	73	74	60	59

Source: Breton, 1972: 138.
Reproduced by permission of Information Canada.

Table 3-7

Proportion of boys in sample aspiring to high-status occupations, related to occupational status of father.

Father's Status	% Aspiring to High Status Occupations
High	78.9 (47,849)
Medium	67.0 (73,893)
Low	56.2 (38,804)

Source: Breton, 1972: 232. Reproduced by permission of Information Canada.

Also similar to the findings of other researchers, Breton shows that the proportion of boys aspiring to high-status occupations varies with region and with community size. As our previous discussion would predict, the Maritimes have a lower incidence of high-status occupational aspirations, and smaller communities have a lower incidence of high aspirations (Tables 3-8 and 3-9).

Given the previously described obstacles and advantages to social mobility in Canada, such as living conditions and support in the home or the qualifications of teachers, variations in aspirations by social class, including region and rural versus urban residence, are quite unremarkable. Lower-class children are in a very real sense socialized to aim much lower than their middle-class counterparts. The socialization is vested in the every-day experiences of the classes, and serves to maintain the system of social stratification.

Table 3-8

Proportion of boys aspiring to high status occupations, by region

Region	% Aspiring to High Status Occupations
Atlantic	56.3 (15,620)
Quebec	70.0 (71,019)
Ontario	67.6 (59,810)
West	65.9 (47,776)

Source: Breton, 1972: 232.
Reproduced by permission of Information Canada.

Table 3-9

Proportion of boys aspiring to high status occupations, by community size

Community Size	% Aspiring to High Status Occupations
250,000 or larger	76.9 (1,573)
10,000 to 249,999	67.7 (1,410)
Smaller than 10,000	53.6 (1,190)

Source: Breton, 1972: 232.
Reproduced by permission of Information Canada.

The socialization occurs in the home, among peers, in the neighbourhood or community, and in the schools themselves. Lower-class and middle- or upper-class parents will have different attitudes toward formal education and different skills to impart to their children. Similarly, there are different economic demands and pressures to earn money rather than to study; education may be free, but not all implements are, while more important, forgone income of children in school may be perceived as vital to the standard of living of a lower-class family. The middle class advantage extends to the classroom. Rather than neutralize or overcome family (class), neighbourhood, or regional influences, the school crystallizes them and reinforces them.

In the classroom the lower-class child is less likely to perform up to middle-class-dominated school expectations, either in skills or in decorum — each related to home experience. Poorer performance, and perhaps early failure, become self-perpetuating, for the child becomes labelled as "not too bright", a "failure", and perhaps a "troublemaker". Eventually, as the child perceives this teacher attitude, also shared by his middle-class peers, his or her self-image becomes consistent with the label, as do his aspirations and achievements. In aspiring to low levels, the student with poor grades, usually from the lower class where he is less well prepared to earn good grades, is simply conforming to the expectations of family, friends, and teachers. (Forcese and Siemens, 1965: 23.)

Even given the ideal school situation of the genuinely unbiased teacher, and even given a student doing well academically, evidence suggests that lower-class children tend to think that the teacher views them unfavourably. That is, whatever the teacher's actual attitudes, the lower-class child perceives the teacher to be hostile, thereby affecting the student self-image and attitude to school. (Davidson and Lang, 1960: 107-118.)

Also relating to self-image and aspirations are teacher attention and encouragement. The teacher is in effect being rewarded by the "good" student who does what is expected and makes fewer demands, including disciplinary demands. In turn, therefore, the "good" student is further encouraged by the teacher, whereas the "poor" student, usually from the lower class, is further neglected despite needing greater assistance, thus reinforcing inadequate performance. The student who is not receiving any rewards or benefits in the school is then apt to turn to non-academic pursuits in order to win acceptance of peers or school authorities; these activities might be athletic, or delinquent. The import of teacher and school influence was identified in a Manitoba survey of senior high school students (Forcese and Siemens, 1965) and similarly in a Halifax study. In the latter it was concluded that school environment, including teacher attitudes (as perceived and in fact) and student sub-cultures, were more important than family environment in influencing continued school attendance. (Or, 1970.) This is so in the sense that extraordinary teacher encouragement and support may overcome the handicaps of class background.

Rural students experience situations similar to the urban lower class in the "alien" nature of the school environment. They, too, experience fewer opportunities to deal in abstractions, fewer models of high-status roles or occupations, lower incomes and greater demands to "work" and earn money, less well-trained teachers and often poorer school facilities. Where the facilities are comparable to urban schools, as in the "consolidated" schools, they are often utilized only at the expense of additional hours spent in busing to the school. Consequently, lower aspirations are also characteristic of rural students.

Class, Aspirations, and Achievement

If we examine the extent to which aspirations and expectations are in fact realized, we find that the greater probability of aspiration achievement is among middle- and upper-class students. Note that this means that lower-class students are less likely to have high aspirations in the first place, but even given high aspirations, are less apt to fulfil them.

For example, one of the few studies to follow up on reported aspirations by checking achievements was conducted in Manitoba. There it had been found that lower-class students were less likely to aspire to university. In the follow-up it was found that only to a slight extent did more of the high-aspiration upper- and middle-class students go on to university than high-aspiration lower-class students. The researchers were of the view that the pool of high-aspiring lower-class students was too small for a greater class distinction in achievement to show up. That is, the bulk of lower-class students had already fallen out of the educational system, such that the few lower-class students remaining were something of an élite. (Siemens and Jackson, 1965: 18-19.)

Clearer findings are reported from a large research project still under way under the direction of Bernard Blishen and John Porter. Students in Ontario near the end of their grade 12 in 1971 were surveyed, and then re-questioned more than a year later in the fall of 1972, by which time they should have completed Ontario grade 13, the final year of high school. When they were re-contacted, it was found that of the 2119 students reached, 53.9 per cent had left school without completing grade 13. (McRoberts, 1973: 6.) Not all of these entered the labour force. But in the original survey in 1971, only 25 per cent of the students had expected to enter the labour force, whereas by 1972, 47.7 per cent had actually done so. Only 29.5 per cent of the total follow-up sample had gone on to university, where in the original survey, 40 per cent had expected to do so.

When these results were examined by social class, it was found that twice as great a proportion of middle- and upper-class students had entered university than lower-class students. (McRoberts, 1973: 33-34.)

If we consider the structure of the Ontario high school system at the time of the research, we find that it consisted of four-year and five-year streams. The latter, since it included grade 13, in fact constituted a "university-prep" within the high schools. Notably, there is disproportionate class representation in each of the two streams. Middle- and upper-class students cluster in the five-year stream, to the extent of more than three quarters of middle and upper class students, while lower-class students are approximately evenly divided among the two streams. (McRoberts, 1973: 24; Porter, Porter and Blishen, 1973: 58-60; Gilbert and McRoberts, 1974: 42.) The data are reported in Table 3-10.

Table 3-10

Student's program by father's occupational status *

	Status						
Program	I	II	III	IV	V	VI	Total
5—year	86	83	74	69	51	51	65
4—year	14	16	26	30	43	49	35
Number	(178)	(212)	(289)	(534)	(1,021)	(299)	(2,530)

*Source: Reprinted with the permission of B.R. Blishen and John Porter, from their study of Ontario High School Students.
Cited in: Gilbert and McRoberts, 1974; 1975.
Marion R. Porter, John Porter and Bernard R. Blishen, *Does Money Matter? Prospects for Higher Education*: Toronto, Institute for Behavioural Research, York University, 1973.

The disproportionate class representation persists even when I.Q. is controlled. Although a relatively high number of lower-class students of high I.Q. were in the five-year stream, at the same time, even low I.Q. upper- and middle-class students were in the five-year program in high proportion. (McRoberts, 1973: 25.) (See Table 3-11.) Moreover, when it

Table 3-11

Proportion of Ontario Grade 12 respondents in five-year program, by social class and by I.Q.

	Class		
	Upper	Middle	Working
Mental Ability			
High	94.7	86.2	79.8
Moderate	79.4	79.8	56.6
Low	66.0	50.3	38.5

Source: McRoberts, 1973: 33.

came to "cashing in" the five-year program, even among the high I.Q. students only 43 per cent entered university, and these were largely the non-lower-class students. (McRoberts, 1973: 26.)

It should be noted that we are not assuming I.Q. scores to be a literal measure of intelligence or an objective and valid measure of mental ability. As we shall discuss, short of the extremes of genius and idiocy, I.Q. tests may better measure social advantages and learned social responses appropriate to the middle-class schools of the dominant ethnic group. Thus such tests by their nature, reduce the number of working-class students who score highly. However, the previous data demonstrate that even if lower-class students manage to do well against the middle-class definition of intelligence, they are still relatively unlikely to go on to higher educational and occupational achievement. Such findings are indicative of the role of schools in the stratification system. We recapitulate the interaction between class, home, and school in the following pages, stressing that the result is the retardation of lower-class mobility and the maintenance of middle- and upper-class advantage.

Home and School

There is no question but that formal educational opportunity is critical insofar as Canadian employers have come to emphasize academic credentials as indicators of suitability for employment. Educational institutions have come to serve as gatekeepers to "success"; the emphasis is, in effect, upon gatekeeping, rather than facilitating mobility. Significantly, where formal education may permit some mobility in Canada, it does not secure equal opportunity for all classes in Canada. Some lower-class students make it through the schools and universities, but generally the educational institutions have served the function of perpetuating the relative advantages of middle- and upper-class persons, ensuring that they will inherit the class standing of their fathers.

We have seen some of the data demonstrating variable aspirations and achievement by class, indicating that lower-class children tend not to succeed in school and complete university. Some observers are quite happy to ascribe this differential achievement to the intelligence of students, noting that lower-class children have lower I.Q.s. The implication is, of course, that such I.Q. scores are adequate measures of intelligence and indicate hereditary differences; it is because of lesser intelligence that lower-class students do less well, and why they and their families are in fact lower class. A literal interpretation of such test scores permits such a view, for consistently, in fact, lower-class children do less well on I.Q. tests, even where some attempt has been made to standardize for class and ethnic background. But sociologists find contrary data more convincing, and take the view that I.Q. tests are very imperfect and crude indicators of innate ability, as distinct from social experience. I.Q. tests reflect middle-class experiences and learned abilities, including symbolic manipulation. Lower-class children do less well because the tests do not measure lower-class meanings and skills, and because they are usually administered in a middle-class setting — the school. The middle-class person whose "native tongue" is English, or French in Quebec, will do better. Thus, deriving from his examination of such I.Q. bias against Mexican-American children, the American sociologist John Garcia refers to the administration and reliance upon I.Q. tests as the "conspiracy of the ruling class", for they serve to perpetuate dominant class definitions of performance and existing inequities. (Garcia, 1972; Kerchoff, 1972: 73-74.)

The schools, as we have previously argued, capitalize upon the entering advantage of non-lower-class students, not from some conscious and malicious conspiracy, but simply from a privileged class ethnocentrism. Our schools are operated by middle-class school boards, administrators, and teachers. In Anglophone Canada they are characteristically of British-Canadian background. In a sample of high school teachers in Hamilton, Jones found that the majority of teachers came from families of above-average socio-economic status, and most were English or second-generation Canadian. (Jones, 1963: 537.) They quite naturally expect behaviour consistent with their own middle-class experiences. For example, features of middle-class family life, but not the lower class, such as promptness, cleanliness, and non-agressive behaviour, are realistic expectations only of middle-class children, not working-class and especially slum children. Yet the absence of such traits often elicits disapproval and punishment of an overt sort, as well as a more subtle biasing of teacher attitude and behaviour.

Similarly, related to the I.Q. bias is the matter of school preparation. The middle-class child, before entering school and throughout his school years, lives in a supportive and compatible environment. Prior to school he will acquire verbal and reading skills, either by deliberate emphasis or merely as a normal feature of day-to-day living. There are books and magazines, papers, pens, and pencils all readily available in the middle-class home, used by the parents, and their use by the children taught and encouraged. The parents will themselves be quite well educated and literate, and will hold down jobs where intellectual activity is required, thereby standing as role models for the children. In fact, more than simply having occupational role models, the upper- and middle-class child will frequently have deliberate tutoring by parents or professionals. Increasingly formal pre-school training is becoming the norm. Nursery schools, pre-schools, kindergartens, are costly advantages not routinely available to lower-class families, while those already privileged use them to provide their children with an accelerated instruction in school-related skills and familiarity with the school environment. (Kerchoff, 1972: 60-79.)

In addition, influencing the attitudes of their children, it is quite common for lower-class parents to be suspicious and even hostile to schools. Thus, not only do lower-class households lack the tools of education, but they also lack supportive attitudes. In fact, a lower-class child who too strenuously attempts to succeed at school activities will meet not only the ridicule and opposition of peers, but often also of parents.

Home environment and school environment interact to reinforce non-achievement for the lower-class child, and high performance for the middle- and upper-class child. There is differential advantage from the time children enter first grade. The middle-class child will perform in the expected manner, for he has already been taught to do so. The middle-class child comes to be viewed as more intelligent and is rewarded, by school and by parents. But the lower-class child, also performing as expected and consistent with learned experience, does not do well and is "stigmatized" as a failure. This definition is passed on, in teacher conversations and school records, and is also communicated to the child who comes to view himself as a failure. Failure comes to be a self-fulfilling prophecy.

It is ironic that it is the lower-class child who can benefit more from teacher support, yet who is least apt to receive it.

> . . .the teacher's influence upon lower class children is potentially much greater than her influence upon middle class children. The latter generally receive assistance and encouragement at home, and are thus better able to be academically successful *in spite* of the kind of teaching they experience. (Kerchoff, 1972: 74)

Failing exceptional support at home or at school, lower-class children tend to drop out of school as early as the law permits, often failing to complete high-school matriculation and infrequently going on to post-high-school programs, especially university. Earlier, in Table 3-1, we saw that the low-income regions of Canada are those with the lowest school retention rates. In Table 3-12, we find illustrated the relative class segregation in educational institutions in Canada for 1951, simply by looking at young people aged 14 to 24, living at home and attending an educational institution. The higher the class, the higher the proportion in school.

If we look at university attendance by class levels, we find a similar relationship, except that the upper class (Blishen class 1) is less well represented in university than the upper-middle class (Blishen class 2). Other than middle-class families, the children of skilled workers are

Table 3-12

Proportion of young people 14-24 in school by Blishen class levels, 1951

Class	Percentage
1	71.0
2	55.2
3	50.6
4	45.6
5	38.9
6	38.2
7	34.8

Reproduced by permission of University of Toronto Press from John Porter, "The Vertical Mosaic", Toronto, University of Toronto Press, 1965, p. 180.

Table 3-13

Proportion of university students in Canada by Blishen class levels, 1951

Class	Percentage
1	11.0
2	34.9
3	4.8
4	7.1
5	19.7
6	5.8
7	11.4

Reproduced by permission of University of Toronto Press from John Porter, "The Vertical Mosaic", University of Toronto, Press, 1965, p. 186.

best represented in university, but not nearly in proportion to their over-all number in the labour force (Table 3-13).

The significance of these 1951 data rests in their comparison with more recent information; there is little change in pattern. When we take educational level of parents as an indicator of class, we find a similar relationship between class of parents and education of children in 1966. If both parents are university educated, then 51 per cent of their children will be university educated, as contrasted to 18.8 per cent of the children of parents educated only to the secondary level, and 4.8 per cent of the children of primary-educated parents. Where one parent is university educated and the other secondary educated, 35.8 per cent (father university) and 38.4 per cent (mother university) of the children achieve university education. Quite dramatically, where one parent is university educated and the other only primary educated, the difference in parental background appears so great that children are not provided the support needed to reach and complete university, and the proportions drop to 17.25 per cent (father university) and 24.8 per cent (mother university) (Table 3-14).

Table 3-14

Educational level by educational level of parents, 1966[1]

Parents' Level of Education		Level of Education of Children			
Father	Mother	Total	University	Secondary	Elementary
		per cent			
University	University	100.0	51.0	46.1	2
Secondary	Secondary	100.0	18.8	74.9	6.3
Elementary	Elementary	100.0	4.8	42.9	52.3
University	Secondary	100.0	35.8	59.7	4.5
Secondary	University	100.0	38.4	57.6	2
University	Elementary	100.0	17.2	64.3	18.5
Elementary	University	100.0	24.8	59.7	15.5
Secondary	Elementary	100.0	10.3	68.9	20.8
Elementary	Secondary	100.0	9.8	70.1	20.1

[1] *Respondents 14 years and over.*
[2] *Sample too small for reliable estimate.*
Source: Perspectives Canada, 1974, Table 4.35, p. 89.
Reproduced by permission of Information Canada.

We may also look directly at relationships between occupation of father and the participation of children in post-secondary education. In 1968-1969, the greater proportions of students taking some post-secondary education had fathers in the managerial, professional/technical, and clerical/sales occupations, that is, upper-middle to middle-class occupations (Table 3-15).

Similarly, if we examine family income and post-secondary enrolment, we find a consistent increase in the proportion of post-secondary students by family income groups. The range extends from lower income families of less than $2000 per annum income with a negligible 1.4 per cent of university graduates, to families of $10 000 and over with 39.2 per cent of the graduates in 1968-1969 (Table 3-16).

Finally, we may also note that an ethnic bias enters educational achievement, as we would expect given the relationship between social class and ethnicity as discussed in Chapter Two. We know that in Canada middle- and upper-class Canadians tend to be from British-Canadian backgrounds, with a well-established Jewish middle-class

Table 3-15

Occupation of parents of post-secondary students, 1968-69

	Occupation of father	Occupation of all males in labour force	Occupation of mother	Occupation of all females in labour force
			per cent	
Managerial	22	12	2	4
Professional and technical	16	11	7	17
Clerical and sales	21	13	14	40
Craftsmen and production workers	6	32	1	10
Labourers	9	6	2	1
Service	6	7	2	23
Farming	9	12	2	3
Other	11	7	70[1]	2
TOTALS	100	100	100	100

[1] *Includes housewives, (61 per cent).*

Source: Perspective Canada, 1974: 90, Table 4:36.
Reproduced by permission of Information Canada.

Table 3-16

Post-secondary attendance by parental income, academic year 1968-69[1]

Family income group	Graduated from university 1968-69	University under-graduate	Community colleges and CEGEPs	Total
		per cent		
Less than $2,000	1.4	1.0	0.9	1.0
$ 2,000—$2,999	5.1	4.1	4.3	4.2
3,000— 3,999	6.7	4.9	6.3	5.2
4,000— 4,999	4.8	6.2	8.8	6.5
5,000— 6,999	21.1	20.7	29.7	22.0
7,000— 9,999	21.7	24.6	27.0	24.8
10,000 and over	39.2	38.5	23.0	36.3
	100.0	100.0	100.0	100.0
Median family income	$8,502	8,600	7,003	8,349

[1] *Excluding senior matriculation and foreign students.*
Reproduced by permission of Information Canada.

minority. Reflecting both education in Canada and the educational levels of immigrants admitted to the country, for the male non-agricultural labour force in 1961, the highest proportions of university educated are of Jewish and British descent, and the lowest is Italian (Table 3-17).

Table 3-17

Ethnicity and educational achievement of the male non-agricultural labour force, 1961

Ethnic Descent	% University Educated
British	12.5
French	6.3
German	9.2
Italian	3.0
Jewish	25.5
Ukrainian	7.9
Other	10.9
All origins	10.1

Source: *Canada, 1969: 26*
Reproduced by permission of Information Canada.

To summarize, by whatever the indicator, all data suggest that children inherit the social classes of their families in Canada. Rather than overcome such inheritance, the school system reinforces it.

Lower Class Occupational Mobility

The environmental and educational restraints given, the extent of lower-class mobility is inevitably slight. For example, in his study of a working-class neighbourhood in Toronto, Crysdale found that very few children of manual workers improved upon their father's occupational status. He estimated that about two out of five may have jobs superior to their fathers', but usually still within the same social class level. Moreover, about the same number of sons as improved their positions actually occupied lower positions, or were downwardly mobile. (Crysdale, 1968: 2.) In general, therefore, there was no class mobility; where there was improvement in occupational position across generations, it was not so much in terms of higher status jobs as in better wages, fringe benefits, and greater job security, while still at the level of manual occupations. (Crysdale, 1968: 296.)

Even where mobility occurs, for persons from the lower classes and economically deprived regions, there are traditional occupations that are accessible. For example, teaching, social work, and particularly nursing have been defined as middle-class occupations offering opportunity to lower-class persons. As such, they are viewed as the least desirable middle-class vocations for middle-class persons. Moreover, having taken up such professions, lower-class persons are more apt to make careers of them, as opposed to leaving them after a brief time. This pattern was demonstrated in a study of nursing careers in Halifax, where nurses of middle-class origins did not persist in their careers to the extent of their colleagues of lower-class origins. (Hoare, 1969.)

Generally, therefore, success even where it is attained by the person of lower-class family is limited. Relatively few persons escape their class of origin, and when they do, it is characteristically by way of the less prestigious and less financially rewarding professions.

Conclusions

The key to whether a modern industrial society is open and extending mobility opportunities sufficient to overcome ascribed social class membership is the educational system. If lower-class persons are succeeding in schools and universities, we have indication of an open-class system. (Parkin, 1972: 111.) The educational system would then be functioning in keeping with the meritocratic ideal and an egalitarian ethic. But in Canada the educational system has not been working in such a fashion. By region, by ethnic group, and by social class, the probability of academic success and occupational entré are unequal. Upper- and middle-class students are permitted to meet the meritocratic definition of equal competition; lower-class students are not.

The remarkable and rare entrepreneur aside, occupational success has increasingly become dependent upon educational screening. This was to have been the means of overcoming the inheritance of social class. However, as presently constituted the educational system favours the already privileged, and screens out the already disadvantaged. Rather than defeating stratification, formal education is a cause of persisting and increasingly rigid stratification. One is given no choice but to "make it" in the school system if one is to secure superior status. But as the means to meritocratic egalitarianism, educational organization has acted to secure meritocracy for the meritocrats, or middle-class status for the middle class.

4

CLASS, LIFE STYLE, AND BEHAVIOUR

Class as Reality

Whatever the inadequacies of measurement, it is clear that classes are not mere artefacts of definition. They are real and integral aspects of Canadian society. Intrinsically economic, they are in Canada meshed with ethnic and regional differentiation. The classes that exist in Canada may be estimated by resort to labour force information or education such as we have been doing, although it must be recalled that such data do not fully express the extent of poverty or the magnitude of inherited corporate wealth. However, these data do reflect the relative economic advantages in Canadian society, in that educational qualifications and occupational roles have been associated with varying levels of economic return. Such economic acquisition is translated into degrees of prestige and power, but is no less fundamentally economic for that.

The essential reality of class consists not merely of existence, but also of persistence. The advantages of one generation are passed to the next, and wealth and power are consolidated. This is particularly so of the closed upper class of owners, persons who maintain control of major industrial resources and corporate wealth, including Canada's major financial institutions. This economic élite has become increasingly impenetrable. But we have stressed rather more the inheritance of middle-class advantage, for this is a more salient, if no more important, dimension of stratification for the majority of Canadians. The élite may be closed to the mobility aspirant, but so too is the middle class of professional and managerial occupations and remuneration increasingly closed to lower-class mobility. Especially instrumental in this regard is the educational system. To a large extent the upper-class child may be safely indifferent to formal academic credentials, for his career, wealth, and security are ensured by virtue of the family's ownership of industrial property and massive capital accumulation. But the non-propertied person lacking inherited wealth depends upon a professional or white-collar career, the basis of which is educational credentials. Education secures and maintains a middle-class occupation, including an improved middle-class position over that of one's parents.

The lower-class individual, we have seen, tends to be unable to compete for educational certification and middle-class occupational standing. Just as the middle-class person tends to be incapable of achieving upper-class status because of the enormity of inherited relative disadvantage, so too in structural position and learned skills is the lower-class individual unable to overcome the inherited advantage of the middle class. Sheer economic difficulties and learned attitudes militate against successful competition in middle-class-dominated educational institutions and career sectors. Thus, inherited wealth and learning opportunities secure the perpetuation of social classes. Classes do not consist of individuals differentially achieving on the basis of ability, but of individuals inheriting the advantages or disadvantages of their parents before them.

Canada, we are told, is an affluent society. Most people reading these remarks would be of the privileged middle class and in quest of a credit against the requisite university degree. We would share a relative satisfaction with our life styles and prospects, and some pride in our society. We would perhaps take satisfaction in the conviction that no one starves to death or dies of untreated disease in Canada. But unfortunately such a conviction although literally correct would require qualification. Even in terms of such fundamentals as food and health care, class in Canada is not just a matter of some people having somewhat more or somewhat different, but of some people having too much, and others insufficient.

The "welfare state" secures basic sustenance, shelter, medical care, and a measure of security for all Canadians, administrative malpractice aside. But this is by no means the same as all Canadians being well fed and adequately nourished, well and adequately sheltered, or well and adequately cared for medically. Nothing could be less true. And even if it were, as we shall take up in Chapter Five, the existence of welfare programs in conjunction with the existence of a class structure both concedes and contributes to the greater rigidity of that class structure, however humane such welfare programs might be.

Class and Health

It is readily apparent that some Canadians spend virtually all their income in order to secure food, clothing, and residence, while others have an income large enough to enable them to consume a massive volume of luxury items. In Chapter Two we considered definitions of poverty that were dependent upon income level and proportion of income available for non-necessities. Canadians who exist at or near the subsistence level as so defined in our society may be markedly richer than in many nations, but they are no less deprived in contrast to their more privileged fellow citizens, or deprived relative to some national ideal.

A fundamental indicator of class disparity is quality of health care.

The poor eat less nutritious foods and are not as well cared for medically. Health care is now guaranteed in Canada; yet the facilities are not equally available. Nor are drugs, which are not covered by government programs except under stringent welfare conditions, a deficiency particularly to the disadvantage of the aged. For the poor, seemingly trivial factors such as the cost and the difficulty of transportation in aid of economical shopping, or reaching physicians and hospitals, are significant. Especially with regard to medical treatment, time lost at work, or its prospect, is also of considerable import.

Generally there is a reluctance and sufficient difficulty involved on the part of the poor in obtaining health care, such that middle- and upper-class persons actually utilize medical facilities and services to a greater extent than do lower-class persons. Not only will the upper classes more often seek and receive medical assistance, they are more apt to secure specialized medical treatment. Ultimately, in association with poorer nutrition and often poorer working conditions, this means a higher morbidity rate for lower class persons, as was suggested in data collected in Calgary four years after the inauguration of health care insurance. (Fraser, 1968.)

Similarly, dental treatment is not universally available in Canada. The degree of dental care increases dramatically with the class level of Canadians. In 1950-1951 low-income persons in Canada utilized physicians and dentists roughly one half as often as high-income persons. (Canada, 1960: 50-55.) Medical treatment for lower-class persons has since improved with nation-wide medicare, as confirmed in the Calgary study. (Fraser, 1968.) But for reasons noted above, class variation persists, especially in dental care in the absence of any comparable program of dental insurance and the very high costs of dental treatment.

These variations relate to the regional and the rural-urban differences that we have previously outlined. There are far more doctors and dentists, for example, in urban areas. By major region, as shown in Table 4-1 and in Figures 4-1 and 4-2 British Columbia and Ontario have the greatest number of physicians and dentists relative to population, while the Maritimes (Nova Scotia excepted) and the Yukon and Northwest Territories are least well served. Also poorly served is Saskatchewan, still largely a rural province and perhaps also still suffering the effects of a medical exodus in the 1960s, a topic we shall take up in Chapter Five. Over all, the industrialized and prosperous regions of Canada have the bulk of the medically qualified personnel. Similarly, when we examine individual expenses for dental services, we find the greater expenditures in the economically developed regions of Canada, reflecting in part the higher costs of such services, but more basically, the more frequent utilization of dentists. Noteworthy is the stability of relative expenditures over the decade from 1961 through 1971 (Table 4-2).

The availability of medical and dental treatment is not merely a matter of the number and accessibility of physicians and dentists. Also

Figure 4-1

Population per Physician, 1971(1)

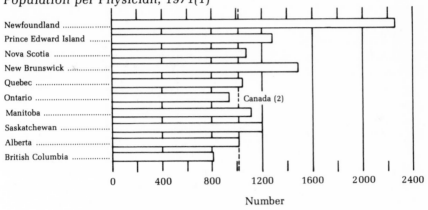

(1) Estimated number of Active Fee Physicians, see Concepts and Definitions.
(2) Canada includes the Yukon and the Northwest Territories.

Perspective Canada, p. 56
Chart 3:35

Table 4-1

Regional differences in provision of health, manpower and hospital facilities, Canada and provinces, 1968-1970

	Population per Physician, 1970	Population per Dentist, 1968	Hospital Beds per 1000 Population, 1970
Newfoundland	1118	9236	7.8
Prince Edward Island	1134	4231	10.4
Nova Scotia	744	4720	9.6
New Brunswick	1102	5531	10.2
Quebec	682	4031	10.0
Ontario	654	2697	9.6
Manitoba	701	3627	10.0
Saskatchewan	804	5005	11.2
Alberta	720	3353	12.3
British Columbia	627	2519	9.5
Yukon & Northwest Terr.	1150	9200	12.6
Canada	692	3319	10.0

Source: Canada 1972; Canada 1970 (cited in Manzer, 1974)
Reproduced by permission of Information Canada.

pertinent is the availability of specialized medical skills. Here again the advantage is to the urban industrialized regions of Canada. A medical or dental career is most lucrative in the cities, as well as more prestigious within the professions. That alone would serve to attract specialists. But in addition, specialization requires a considerable

Figure 4-2

Population per Dentist, 1971

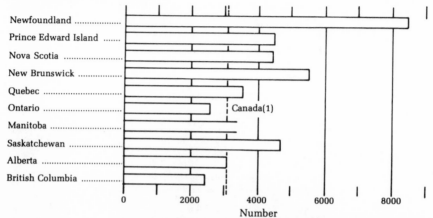

(1) Canada includes the Yukon and the Northwest Territories
Perspectives Canada, p. 57   Chart 3:37
Reproduced by permission of Information Canada

Table 4-2

Expenditure per person on dentists' services[1]

	1961	1966	1971
CANADA	6.39	7.02	8.07
Newfoundland	1.98	2.20	2.79
Prince Edward Island	3.93	4.43	4.70
Nova Scotia	3.48	4.59	4.66
New Brunswick	3.43	3.69	4.21
Quebec	3.97	4.61	5.08
Ontario	8.55	9.36	10.70
Manitoba	6.65	6.26	7.58
Saskatchewan	5.27	5.49	5.36
Alberta	7.00	7.88	8.97
British Columbia	9.85	9.87	11.70

[1] *Annual expenditure in constant 1961 dollars.*
Source: Perspective Canada, 1974: 57, Table 3.36.
Reproduced by permission of Information Canada.

population, and elaborate facilities, including instructors; for the latter, the teaching hospitals of the large metropolitan centres are vital.

Thus, medical care may be guaranteed all Canadians, but the ease and promptness of treatment, and the expertise, are not equally guaranteed. The regional distribution of skilled personnel, and the attitudes of the members of the social classes, make for a disparity of health care services.

Of Canada's population, more than any other group the native peoples suffer from disease, poor nutrition, and inadequate health care. A good indicator is the rate of infant mortality, which for Canada as a whole in the years 1961-1963 was 28.6 deaths per 1000 population. For Indians the rate was 65.5 per 1000, and for Eskimos the rate was 178.9. (Canada, 1965: 52.) Or, if we take as our indicator of quality of life and health care the incidence of tuberculosis, we find enormous variations. The Eskimo (Inuit) in 1971 suffered a rate of tuberculosis approximately 25 times as high as all of Canada, and the Indians a rate about six times as high. Incredible as these statistics are, they are down sharply from the rates of 1965, when the Inuit rate of tuberculosis per 100 000 population was 846 as contrasted to the total Canadian rate of 25 (Table 4-3).

Table 4-3

Tuberculosis among Inuit, Registered Indians, and other Canadians

	Total Canada	Inuit	Indian	Other
		rate per 100,000 pop.		
1965	25	846	163	22
1966	23	882	181	20
1967	23	1020	161	20
1968	22	810	177	21
1969	21	1093	166	18
1970	18	672	125	16
1971	18	496	122	17

Source: *Perspectives Canada*, Table 3:14, p. 43, 1974.
Reproduced by permission of Information Canada.

In addition to health, there are other indicators of the differential well-being of Canadians, some rather more frivolous. For example, of a serious nature, we saw in Chapter One the regional variation in the quality of shelter, a variation we know to be related to social class. For example, in 1968 the percentage of homes with flush toilets, including those shared with other families, was 84.4 per cent for those with household average incomes of under $1000 per annum, as contrasted to the national average of 94.3 per cent. Or, for this same low-income group, the incidence of central heating by furnace was 63.7 per cent, while the national average was 76.9 per cent. What is not apparent in these figures is that lower-income homes are also older, and they are more crowded. (Canada, 1968: 42.) Thus, in addition to the sheer income deprivation of some Canadians are tangible and fundamental differences in the quality of life, in terms of facilities that middle-class Canadians take for granted and that we would expect to be universal in an affluent welfare state.

Figure 4-3   *Families Reporting Selected Expenditures, by Income Group, 1969*

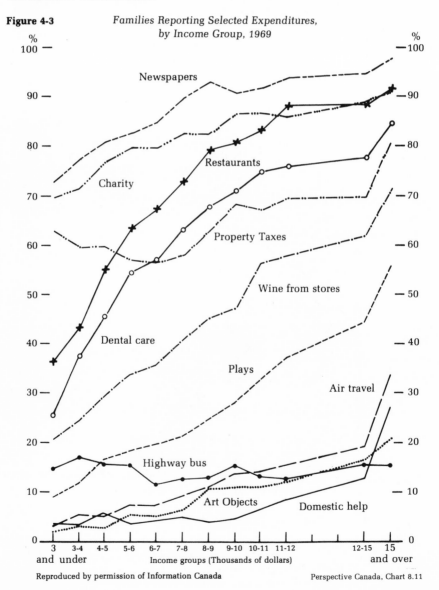

Perspective Canada, Chart 8.11

When we go on to consider luxury or consumer items, such as travel, restaurant use, art, wine, and entertainment, the differences in Canadian life-style are, of course, magnified. Naturally the expenditure and consumption related to such non-subsistence commodities increases with income level (Figure 4-3).

The regional variations in family consumption are also conspicuous. Figure 4-4 shows the amount of disposable income by region, demonstrating the previously remarked pattern of greater income in urban areas and in industrialized provinces such as Ontario. The great con-

Figure 4-4

Patterns of Family Expenditure by Province, 1969

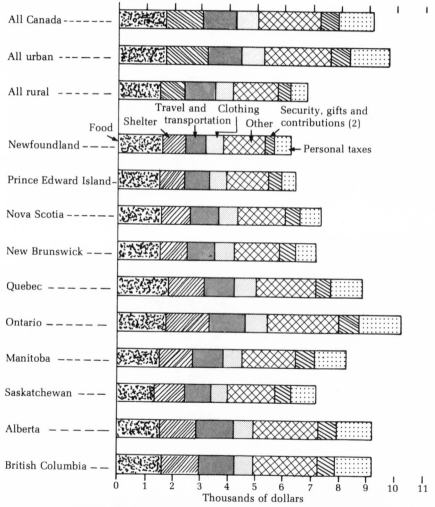

(1) For the definition of the family see Concepts and Definitions.
(2) Includes life insurance, unemployment insurance and pension plans.
Reproduced by permission of Information Canada

trast is with the Maritimes, as we have already seen against other criteria. It should be additionally noted that this greater non-subsistence spending also means greater spending on security-related items, such as supplementary health care insurance, dental insurance, life insurance, and pension plans. The purchase of such security is a basic advantage of non-lower-class Canadians and often is a routine "fringe benefit" of employment and not a cost against salary.

We need not be too literal in examining such expenditures. Volume of consumption is not synonymous with quality of life or some concept of "happiness". But to the extent that there are systematic regional and class differences in non-subsistence disposable incomes, we may reasonably infer that some Canadians are better able to enjoy and to fulfil their lives than are others.

Class and Criminal Deviance

If lower-class persons are socialized to expect consumer items of a given quantity, and then the means to the acquisition of such items are inadequate, then it would not be remarkable to find them violating social expectations of behaviour, including those legally defined. Deprived persons might, for example, decide not to work at all because work fails to gain them any advantages. Or they might go through the paces, in a sense, working to rule or to minimum acceptable rate. Conceivably, too, they might resort to illegal means to acquire desired benefits. Many years ago Robert K. Merton suggested that where the learned goals in a society exceeded the legitimate means of achievement for individuals or groups of individuals, people might retreat or withdraw, conform in a ritual-like manner, rebel against the system, or innovate and resort to deviant or non-legitimate means. (Merton, 1957.)

There is no clear evidence suggesting which of these is more probable. In fact, one might question whether the key assumption of learned goals is characteristically operative if we are thinking of lower-class persons; rather, the "culture of poverty" may be taken in part to be the non-salience of such goals. However, it is probably a safe assumption that lower-class Canadians do to some extent value the consumer items to which they do not have access. Yet of Merton's response alternatives, it is safe to note that rebellion is exceedingly rare, and conformity apparently common. Nor is there evidence to suggest that lower-class persons are more apt to engage in criminal deviance than middle- or upper-class persons. Rather, they resort to different and more conspicuous forms of deviance.

In fact, assuming the plausibility of Merton's model, it would predict middle-class criminal deviance more clearly than lower-class deviance, at least insofar as crimes against property as opposed to overt violence or aggression. It is precisely the middle-class person who has high aspirations, as we have seen in Chapter Three, who, in order to realize these aspirations may resort to illegitimate means. The "relative deprivation" of the middle class, as contrasted to the inherited subordination or "culture of poverty" of the lower class, may result in a greater incidence of criminal deviance — deviance of a form particularly suited to middle-class "white collar" opportunities. Also, for the same reason, as we shall go on to discuss, the middle class might better be expected to be the source of political protest and opposition than the more absolutely deprived lower class.

It is commonplace in our society to think of crime, delinquency, drunkenness, drug use, and even gambling as lower-class vices. The view that such deviance is dangerous and undesirable is reflected in our patterns of police enforcement and in our criminal code. In our society we stress the punishment of criminal actions that clash with middle-class conceptions of propriety.

The lower-class individual engaging in criminal activity is resorting to behaviour that violates the property rights of middle-class persons, often by means of the threat or resort to violence. It is the violence, and the conspicuousness of the crime, that meet objections. They are straightforward, non-subtle, and highly visible, readily attracting the intervention of law-enforcement agencies. Robbing a service station, a store, a bank, a home, or an individual are rather conspicuous crimes, though they may be slight in terms of actual dollar values. The public, with the ready aid of the media, are aware of such offences. They are clear-cut violations of Canadian law. Their straightforward nature permits of straightforward police activity, judicial procedure, and punishment, and the offender, as a lower-class person, lacks the influence or prestige to dispute prosecution or arrange intercession on his behalf.

Contrast the nature of lower-class criminal activity to that of the middle class. It is probably fair to say that every reader of this book has committed illegal acts of a criminal nature, whether smoking marijuana, indulging in Canada Customs violations, or committing some acts of fraud or theft. But few will have been apprehended or punished and, therefore, few will have been stigmatized as criminal. The opportunities for middle-class crime are subtle, not highly visible, and not as subject to police supervision. Stealing supplies from the office, accepting gifts for business or government favours, and padding the expense account are not readily detected. Moreover, they are widely considered to be acceptable acts and are even budgeted for by employers. Similarly, more serious middle-class crimes, such as large-scale embezzlement or fraudulent stock deals, are rarely punished with severity, especially relative to lower-class crimes involving far slighter monetary value. The several related factors are: less detectable crime, less subject to police scrutiny or public indignation, and normative toleration of such middle class illegalities, with slight pressure for judicial follow-up.

In 1973 W.J. Fitzsimmons, a former deputy commissioner of the Royal Canadian Mounted Police, commented on the enormity of white-collar crime. In a press report he is quoted as remarking:

> Canadian business lost at least $2.5 billion last year through internal crime. . . "Statistics Canada doesn't require companies to report losses because of white collar crime," Fitzsimmons said in an interview. He said in the United States, statistics show that 37% of business failures are the result of criminal action.
>
> (Montreal Gazette, August 31, 1973)

Thus, lower-class criminal activity is more likely to be taken through the judicial system and appear in statistics; middle-class crime is not.

Similarly, delinquency, drunkenness, drug use are all the more visible and deemed punishable when engaged in by lower-class persons. The lower-class alcoholic is a "drunk" and the middle-class alcoholic a "good guy". Lower-class boys who engage in vandalism are delinquents, while middle-class vandalism is justified with the favoured expression, "Boys will be boys." The very simple point is that in middle-class dominated society, definitions of deviance and the imposition of sanctions are to the disadvantage of lower-class offenders.

Class and Attitudes to Punishment

Perhaps paradoxically, or perhaps reflecting an aspect of what Marx was pleased to call "false consciousness", the lower class are more disposed to favour harsh punishment for criminal acts than are middle-class persons, even when lower-class crime is in question. Lower-class Canadians tend to express less satisfaction and patience with the paraphernalia of "due process". This was illustrated in the reactions of Ottawa residents questioned regarding the kidnapping and death of Pierre Laporte in 1970 and the federal government's response to this "October crisis" in enacting the War Measures Act, dormant since World War II. Lower-class respondents in the survey, identified by education levels, tended to urge prompt and harsh retribution for the "persons responsible" for the death of Laporte, even in some instances suggesting torture of some sort. In contrast, middle-class persons urged restraint and careful prosecution and trial of those "responsible"; given the prospect of a guilty verdict, they were less inclined to suggest capital punishment. (Forcese, Richer, de Vries, and McRoberts, 1971.)

Table 4-4

Attitudes toward due process and punishment after the October crisis, by education

	Education				
	Elementary School	Some High School	Finish High School	Some University	Finish University
By-pass Due Process	72%	55%	52%	26%	22%
Treat as Was Laporte	75%	67%	71%	47%	51%

Source: Forcese, Richer, de Vries, McRoberts, 1971:9.

If we continue to take education as a rough indicator of probable social class, there are other Canadian data that demonstrate the relationship between tolerance or liberal attitudes to civil rights and class membership. Harvey found, in a western Canadian city, that support for freedom of speech increased with educational level. In his sample, 69 per cent of those who had completed a university degree indicated high support, as contrasted to only 12 per cent of those with grade-school education. (Ted Harvey, as cited in Manzer, 1974: 291.)

Other observers have remarked upon attitude or value differences by social class. In particular, lesser patience with due process, a greater inclination to violent or aggressive behaviour and "strong" or "tough"

Table 4-5

Support in a Canadian community for freedom of speech, by level of schooling, 1970

	% Support for Freedom of Speech				
Level of Schooling	Low	Medium Low	Medium High	High	Total
Grade school	40	35	14	12	101
Junior high school	37	33	20	10	100
High school	19	26	33	22	100
Some university	7	14	35	44	100
Completed one university degree	6	5	19	69	99

Source: Ted Harvey, "Attitudes Towards Free Speech in a Canadian Community: A Study of Social, Political and Psychological Correlates", Papers Presented at the Forty-Third Annual Meeting of the Canadian Political Science Association, Volume 3 (mimeo), Table 5.

solutions to problems, and a fatalism have been suggested as characteristics of lower-class persons. (Kluckhohn and Strodtbeck, 1961;
Lipset, 1965.) Summing up these attitudinal characteristics, the notion
of lower-class "authoritarianism" has been suggested by researchers.
The authoritarian is suggested to manifest intolerance of minority
groups and of "unusual" behaviour and an emphasis upon "strong"
leaders and extremist candidates for political office. These attitudes are
hypothesized to be derivative of childhood socialization and perpetuated through generations in the lower class through socialization.
(Adorno *et al.*, 1958; Lipset, 1960; Langton, 1969; Dawson and Prewitt,
1969.) For example, having lived in a downtown working-class neighbourhood in Toronto, Lorimer and Philips remark upon the strict parental controls, as manifest in direct and immediate physical punishment, particularly by the father. (Lorimer and Philips, 1971: 40.) Yet,
apparently favouring strength and resort to force, a derivative of every-
day experience and socialization, it is precisely the lower class of our
society who are most apt to experience such tactics from law-
enforcement agents. In addition, and of considerable importance, it
may be such learned attitudes and responses to environment that contribute to lower-class political behaviour, or its absence.

Class and Politics

Political Participation

The works of Marx and Engels were concerned with the prospect of
classes engaging in political action. The fundamental opposition was
between capitalists who acted to protect their economic dominance,
with the state as their instrument, and the workers who were being
exploited. As they developed an awareness or consciousness of their
shared economic predicament, the working class would become the
vehicle of revolutionary change in society, overthrowing the ruling
class, the state, and class stratification. Only in such political action
would the proletariat actually constitute a class in the full Marxist
sense. Subsequently, Lenin seized on the notion of the "dictatorship of
the proletariat", where the workers form the government and the state
temporarily becomes their instrument until the day it "withers away"
in the interests of the truly egalitarian and classless society.

Persons other than Marxists have expected relationships between
political behaviour and social class, often with some similar expectation of "radical" action by lower-class persons. Yet actual behaviour
seems to contradict such expectations.

It is a very well-established empirical generalization, extending
through all the Western democracies, that lower-class individuals have

a low rate of participation in politics. This is true of memberships in political parties or related organizations, or the simple action of turning out to vote. To put the generalization conversely, the higher the social class, the greater the extent of political participation, including fundamentally the greater probability of any political participation whatsoever. (Milbrath, 1965.) Middle- and upper-class persons, with good reason, view the political process as more efficacious than do lower-class persons; that is, conventional political agencies are perceived to be useful and responsive to their interests. (Milbrath, 1965: 56.) In fact, middle-class persons have the education and the affiliations that make it easier to participate in politics, and to participate effectively. A matter as trivial as the proper and efficient conduct of meetings is often not part of the experience of lower-class persons. Usually there is little organizational experience. In their Toronto working-class study, Lorimer and Philips reported that the only viable voluntary association memberships were in church and labour union. (Lorimer and Philips, 1971: 75-76.)

In Canada, citing work undertaken by John Meisel, Manzer shows that as social class level increases, so does the sense of political efficacy. (Manzer, 1974: 311-313.) Thus lower-class persons feel greater helplessness and, in a sense, a fatalism, regarding their lives as unalterable. Working-class persons are markedly wary of politics and political representatives at all levels of government. They are suspicious of the perceived arbitrary powers of political officers, elected or appointed, and feel neglected and powerless, expressing the view that they simply "can't win". (Lorimer and Philips, 1971: 78-84.)

Class and Voting

This skepticism or apathy is expressed in non-voting. Lower-class persons are less likely to vote than are middle-class persons. (Milbrath, 1965; Lipset, 1960.) For example, in Toronto and Vancouver working-class neighbourhoods, researchers have estimated that approximately one third of the eligible voters actually turn out at the polls. (Lorimer and Philips, 1971: 75-76; Ewing, 1972.) The lower class vote, which some theorists expect to be radical and socialist, is rarely mobilized.

The Marxist-oriented theorists would find such a failure deplorable, an indication of the absence of working-class consciousness, even while at the same time scornful of voting as effective political action at any rate. Others, however, have theorized that a low level of political participation on the part of lower-class voters is desirable insofar as it makes for a "stable" political system. Lipset has argued that lower-class persons, because of their intolerance of civil rights and their preference for the strong leader, are apt to bring about undesirable electoral victories should they in fact vote. (Lipset, 1960.) Normally, when only middle- and upper-class voters turn out, conventional candidates are elected, candidates whom we have already seen in Chapter Two are themselves middle- and upper-class persons and members of established political parties. In Canada the only notable departures from this pattern of higher-status persons successful in politics is in the Social Credit Party and, to some degree, the New Democratic Party. (Forcese and de Vries, 1974.)

In contrast, Lipset continues, when the level of voting turn out increases, probably indicative of an increase in lower-class voting since that is where most non-voters are normally to be found, there is greater probability of the election of persons whom Lipset characterizes as "extremist", those favoured by the working-class authoritarian. The extremist may be of the left or the right. Whether accepting the designation extremist or not, what does seem to occur is greater support for candidates from the non-established parties, third parties such as the Social Credit in Canada.

Related is the expectation that the lower-class vote will tend to favour left-wing or socialist candidates, while the upper-class vote will be more conservative. In fact, some such relationship shows up in western Europe and in the United Kingdom. (Alford, 1963; Lipset, 1960.) But recalling all the while that the extent of lower-class voting tends to be slight in the first place, such lower-class voting as does occur is not so marked and consistent in left-wing preference as the assumption of lower-class preference for socialist policies would predict.

In the United Kingdom there is the well-known phenomenon of the so-called "working-class Tory", referring to lower-class support for the British Conservative Party. (McKenzie and Silver, 1967.) In Canada we similarly find support for other than the New Democratic Party in lower-class ridings, as in David Lewis's 1974 defeat, as well as patterns of self-reported Conservative or Liberal party support by lower-class persons. (Alford, 1963.) In Vancouver civic elections from 1958 to 1970, approximately one third of the lower-class vote went to right-wing candidates. (Ewing, 1972.)

This is not to say that there are no indications of class preferences for specific parties. Some ridings, for example, are traditionally more likely to support one party than another, with neighbourhoods viewed as conservative or socialist strongholds. Especially in civic and provincial elections where riding boundaries are more apt to be coincident with class-segregated neighbourhoods are such patterns evident. One good example that has extended from the civic to the federal level is to be found in North Winnipeg, where left-wing support is well established; at the level of civic elections, not only New Democratic Party but Communist Party candidates have been elected. At the federal level this area has returned New Democratic Party members to Parliament since the pre-World War II period.

However, although such examples do exist at the federal level, available information points to the virtual absence of significant class-related voting. For example, on the basis of several pre-election polls, Alford reports the non-existence of class support in keeping with the traditional left-right expectation. (Alford, 1963.) We may point to the New Democratic Party or the Progressive Conservative Party receiving distinguishable proportions of support from the lower class or the upper class respectively. But in neither instance is it true to say that a class majority supports the party presumed to be of the left or the right, and lower- or upper-class compatible. Rather, in Canada the Liberal Party has established itself as the party of the centre, and has consistently attracted a majority support by apparently appealing to all social classes, including gaining the greatest proportion of support from the voting lower class. (Alford, 1963; Alford, 1964: 211.)

Table 4-6

Trade union voting, federal election 1962

	Union Families	Non-union Families
Conservatives	26%	40%
Liberals	38	38
NDP	22	8

Reproduced by permission of University of Toronto Press from R. Alford, "The Social Bases of Political Cleavage in 1962", in J. Meisel (ed.), "Papers on the 1962 Election", Toronto, University of Toronto Press, 1964.

Unlike elections in Australia or England, where class voting is relatively well established, Alford finds that in Canadian federal elections, regionalism is a better predictor of voting support. (Alford, 1963; 1964.) Porter also argues the import of regional voting in Canada. (Porter, 1965.) As we have previously emphasized, the major regions of Canada are themselves distinguishable ethnically and economically, and they have developed traditional voting allegiances. Thus, New Democratic Party support, federally and provincially, is stronger and more consistent in western Canada, where there is also support for Diefenbaker-style Progressive Conservatives. Ontario is a stronghold of Progressive Conservative Party support, especially at the provincial level, where at time of writing the "big blue machine" still lives on. Quebec consistently supports the federal Liberal Party, which is also the only viable political force provincially at the present time with the demise of the previously powerful Union Nationale. The Maritimes have supported the two old parties, with a Liberal edge, especially pronounced during the heyday of Smallwood's provincial Liberal government.

It seems to be true, as we would argue, that in Canada class interests are being summed up in regional voting at the federal level. However, beyond the Canadian case, other reasons have been put forward to account for the absence of clearer class politics. As a general explanation intended to apply to European as well as to North American politics, Lipset argues that the left-right distinction is too simple to really show up in political behaviour. The distinction does not represent consistent class interests. He offers the distinction between the economic and the civil sectors, and suggest that the lower class may support left-wing policies economically, but in light of working-class authoritarianism, right-wing or conservative civil or social policies are apt to be supported. (Lipset, 1960.) Therefore, the salient issues in an election campaign will determine the direction of lower-class response. Civil issues, such as the issue of the abolition or retention of capital punishment in Canada, invite a conservative lower-class response, as does immigration policy in England.

In addition, Lipset argues that where a two-party system has evolved, ideological and class cleavages tend to disappear from politics. In order to win, each party must generalize its policies and campaign promises in order to appeal to the greatest number of voters. (Lipset, 1960.) Thereby, neither of the two parties becomes a viable class choice, at least not for the lower-class voter. In a similar vein, Alford notes that American and Canadian political parties, unlike those in Australia or in England, have not attempted to develop class identitites. (Alford, 1963.) In particular, except for the New Democratic Party in Canada, there are no firm labour-union ties, even where there may be expectations and prior history of labour-union support as in the case of the Democratic Party in the United States — an expectation that has failed the Democrats in recent presidential elections.

In Canada the New Democratic Party has historically had explicit labour-union affiliations, particularly dating from the 1930s and 1940s, when many socialists held important union positions and encouraged C.C.F. support. (Horowitz, 1968: 54.) However, this affiliation and labour-union financial support have not been readily translated into electoral support of the New Democratic Party by rank-and-file union members. Alford sees Canada and the United States as societies in which the classes have not polarized politically. Moreover, the ruling class has effectively controlled the political process, alternating "competing political élites" from within its ranks. (Alford, 1967.)

We noted in Chapter Two that members of the House of Commons and of the cabinet are largely of high social class. The only deviation from this pattern is in the "third" parties, especially the Social Credit. Much of the minor-party support is agrarian, small business, lower-middle class, and lower-status professionals (for example, teachers). With the exception of such third-party influence and to some extent the

Diefenbaker interlude in the Progressive Conservative Party, the upper classes have effectively monopolized conventional politics. (Forcese and de Vries, 1974.)

Pinard suggests that in particular ruling-class control of politics has been a feature of Quebec political history. The ruling class has dominated decision-making positions and has gained lower-class support. He argues that "negative voting" — that is, lower-class support for right-wing parties and the "conservative and nationalist" character of Quebec political movements — is a function of "élite mediation" of class interests. The upper class in Quebec controls the economic resources and enjoys a value consensus, unlike other societies where there may be conflicting élites within the upper class. Thus the Quebec governing élite, utilizing its control of economic power and the agencies of socialization, such as the church, has manipulated or "translated" lower-class interests into terms consistent with upper-class values and interests. (Pinard, 1970: 107-108.)

Another argument is Lipset's view that Canada is a conservative nation. He states that, in contrast to the United States, Canada has grown out of a foundation in counter-revolution. (Lipset, 1963.) Similarly, although not agreeing that Canada is unmitigatingly conservative, Horowitz suggests that there is in Canadian society a sense of "aristocratic paternalism" in the attitudes of the ruling class, and in the related welfare policies. (Horowitz, 1968.) Because of this genuine conservatism, with its tint of social responsibility, ideologically loaded class-based politics have not been articulated in Canada.

However, in Horowitz's view there is another side to the coin. Because of a clearly defined conservatism in Canada, as contrasted to the characteristic liberalism of the United States (conservatism and liberalism in the sense of European-based ideologies), there has also been room in Canada for a socialist alternative. That is, in the United States the liberal centre emphasis has pre-empted the possibility of either a conservative or a socialist extreme. (Horowitz, 1968: 3-57.) Thus, unlike the United States, Canada has developed a socialist party and has returned that party to office in three provinces, as well as regularly sending a contingent to Ottawa. Lipset and Horowitz both attach importance to Canada's conservative Loyalist origins, but Lipset then sees Canada as inherently conservative, where Horowitz finds a genuine socialist sector among the range of Canadian ideologies. We shall consider each of these views further in evaluating whether in Canada there is at all a class-conscious working-class politics, despite findings stressing the absence of class voting in Canada.

Class and Political Movements

Twenty-five years ago Lipset published an analysis of the emergence of a socialist party in the Canadian West. In 1968, in a preface to a new edition of his work, Lipset suggested that in retrospect he is of the view that he had not been dealing with a socialist party after all, merely an inherently conservative agrarian populism. Thereby the Co-operative Commonwealth Federation (C.C.F.) is rendered consistent with his over-all thesis of Canadian conservatism and greater American egalitarianism. (Lipset, 1963.) Also, in a sense Lipset was expressing a view consistent with more radical theorists — that farmers, as property owners, could not be genuine socialists.

Unlike Lipset, other social scientists have persisted in the view that the C.C.F.-N.D.P. have constituted a genuine socialism, in contrast to the absence of such a party in the United States. As we remarked above, Gad Horowitz suggests that in Canada socialism has developed precisely because of Canadian conservatism as opposed to American liberal centrism. The élitist conservatives in Canada make room for and prompt the development of the counter-ideology of socialism in a kind of dialectic fashion. (Horowitz, 1968.) In addition, he argues that socialist ideology was imported to the United States by "aliens"; that is, by persons who were non-English-speaking immigrants from Europe. The ideology was therefore itself perceived as alien and rejected as "un-American". In Canada, in contrast, socialism was imported principally by immigrants of the same ethnic background as the dominant social class; that is, Englishmen with Fabian and trade union experience. (Horowitz, 1968: 24-29.) This last point is very much consistent with Lipset's initial explanation of the rise of the C.C.F. in Saskatchewan. (1950.)

The initial co-operative and protest movements of the Prairies were certainly not socialist in the European ideological sense. But the agrarian populism evolved into the C.C.F. party and its socialist commitment through the ideological and the organizational input of immigrants from the United Kingdom, as well as from Europe. These were persons with experience in working-class politics and often with affiliations with the working class and social-problems-oriented Methodist religion. (Lipset, 1968: 43.) The first leader of the C.C.F. was J.S. Woodsworth, a Methodist minister; M.J. Coldwell was experienced in British socialism and active in labour organizing. This kind of input was crucial, for, as the literature on social movements suggests, the leaders of the movement lend it a particular stamp. They turned Saskatchewan agrarian protest to socialism, however unlikely socialist farmers might appear. In contrast, American immigration to Alberta, as well as fundamentalist Baptist religious ideology, will have influenced and shaped the ideological character of Alberta agrarian protest, largely identical in origin to Saskatchewan political unrest but becoming translated into support of conservative Social Credit. The conditions and sentiments of economic dissatisfaction and protest were transmuted into one direction or another by the persons actively organizing the protest movements.

Generally political protest movements in Canada have been rural-based, as in the Progressives, the C.C.F., Social Credit, and the Créditistes. And their support has been from a particular class of the rural population. The cross-national literature on social and political movements offers the generalization that the mass support for such movements is from those segments of the population experiencing "relative deprivation". As a region the Prairies were economically precarious. It was not a matter of impoverishment, but of "boom or bust". One year the farm income, depending upon crop and world markets, would be high, another year low. In 1930 the price of a bushel of wheat was $1.50, and in 1932 it was 38 cents, and actually less at the grain elevator. (Gray, 1966: 200)

James Gray relates the story of an Alberta farmer in 1932 who had a good crop but little cash to show for it. As Gray notes, the prairie farmer suffered not merely periodic crop failure such as agriculturalists have always experienced, but often inadequate cash returns even given good harvests. The fluctuation in the price structure, and its utter collapse in the 1930s, was the insufferable feature of prairie farming. Thus, Gray's farmer

> . . .harvested thirty-three bushels to the acre and took it to market when the price of No. 1 Northern was twenty-eight ·and a half cents at the elevator. That autumn had been cold and wet and much of the grain was tough and smutty. This caused the farmer's wheat to be discounted eighteen cents a bushel. Threshing and twine cost seven cents; hauling three cents a bushel. Thus a bumper crop returned its grower *one-half cent* per bushel.
>
> (Gray, 1966: 200)

The rural population was constantly faced with uncertainty and frustrated in any attempt at rational planning and production. For example, investing in expensive eastern-Canadian-manufactured farm equipment in aid of more efficient production came to mean brief use and subsequent re-possession. Farm debts, under the control of Eastern Canadian chartered banks, were enormous. The resentment of the banks, railroads, and manufacturers, all located in the East, was inevitable, and persists to the present. The theory of relative deprivation suggests that precisely because prairie farmers experienced periods of prosperity, as contrasted, for example, to smaller Quebec, Ontario, or Maritime farms, they were moved to "radical" or non-conventional action.

Similarly, within a region the actively dissatisfied are not the people who have always been poor, or those who have been most deprived, but rather people who have experienced some better condition and have found their expectations of continued prosperity frustrated. Lipset (1968) reports that the initial support for the C.C.F. in Saskatchewan came not from the poorest or most marginal farmers, nor the wealthiest, but those whom we might call middle-class farmers. They were perhaps not middle class by urban standards or definition, but relative to their fellows they were persons who were big enough to expect something better, rather than so poor as to despair or so wealthy as to be secure. The boom-or-bust feature of the prairie single-crop agriculture, with its wild fluctuations in farm income, constituted the setting for the farm middle-class dissatisfaction. The provincial and federal governments were viewed as the tool of eastern "big business" interests. In this setting, the C.C.F. became the voice of the Saskatchewan farmer, growing from protest movement to political party to government in 1944, the first socialist government in North America. That year happened to be the year of the highest farm incomes in Saskatchewan history. (Lipset, 1968: 131.)

The people who supported the new party through its emergence to forming the government were the middle-income farmers, with some support from the few workers in Saskatchewan's small cities. The middle-income farmers were those who had supported the Progressives 30 years earlier in the West, as their fellows in Ontario, and generally the persons who have been the basis of rural protest movements. (McCrorie, 1971.) The same kind of people supported the non-socialist protest party in Alberta, leading in 1935 to William Aberhardt's forming a new Social Credit government.

We may take one additional Canadian example in order to underline the rural middle class basis of protest. Almost 30 years after the Social Credit victory in Alberta, Pinard found a similar pattern or rural protest in Quebec. (Pinard, 1971: 94-98.) We underline that the protest occurred after the war, when Quebec had moved out of its agrarian isolation and underdevelopment. In the 1962 federal election many observers were amazed by the support given the Quebec wing of the Social Credit Party of Canada, and their leader, Réal Caouette. The Créditistes were supported by the solid middle range farmer and small town businessman and employees. (Pinard, 1971: 250.) That is, support was from precisely the class of people who were not mired in poverty or rolling in affluence, the class of people who have supported third-party alternatives to the Conservative and Liberal parties through Canadian history.

We stress, therefore, the non-conventional aspect of such political support, in that it departs from "old" party lines. As protest movements, whether coming to be characterized as of the left or of the right, they represent dissatisfaction and attempts at social change. This is not to deny, as Lipset does, that agrarian socialism is any less socialist than some industrially oriented pure form. Without a doubt, C.C.F. government support in Saskatchewan did not represent conventional socialism of European theory or experience. It was not a movement of industrial workers, but of small property-holders, farmers experiencing a fluctuating economy and acquiring facility in co-operative marketing. (Bennett and Krueger, 1971.) Their frustrations were little different from those of their fellow across the Alberta-Saskatchewan border. But insofar as there was a distinctive socialist input from British and European immigrants, from the Methodist and United Churches, and eventually from the study groups formed by such people and well attended through rural Saskatchewan, neither can it simply be dismissed as merely rural populism. The agrarian protest, objecting to eastern Canadian economic control and the insecurity of prairie agriculture, became socialist as much as any collectivity may be said to be so; that is, the party was socialist, and voters supported many of its principles.

Support for a socialist party is opposition to ruling-class interests in Canada, as was support for Social Credit and Diefenbaker "conservatism". It is not a matter of conservative versus socialist ideology, but of opposition radicalism versus upper-class advantage.

We may take from these examples two qualifications to the apparent absence of class politics in Canada. First, we find that there have been politics in opposition to the established parties and the class and regional interests that they represent, in the West and more recently in Quebec. The regions themselves act in a class-like manner. In addition, whether the anti-"establishment" protest is translated into "socialism" or "conservatism", it remains nonetheless the opposition of a subordinate segment of the Canadian population to superior class interests, protest not initially crystallized about any ideological conviction, but deriving from experiences in the regional, ethnic class structure of Canada.

Voting for established parties is conventional and ritual political action in Canadian society. The extent to which Canadians express class sentiments in routinized voting cannot be taken as indicative of class consciousness. Rather, class-based politics, consisting of the actions of industrial and rural workers (among whom we include most individual farm owners), is expressed in non-conventional behaviour, as in the repudiation of the major parties. Such has by no means been a consistent feature of Canadian politics, or even of regions such as the Prairies. But it has been frequent enough to suggest a class-like politics where none is supposed to exist.

Class and Religion

An additional aspect of class behaviour relates to religion. The composition of church congregations is very distinct by social class and represents a structural feature of Canadian society. But more important, and our reason for considering religion here, is the extent to which religious belief and affiliation relate to and reinforce classes and class behaviour.

Sociologists have distinguished religious affiliations by the degree to which they are organized, as opposed to spontaneous, staid in membership acquisition as opposed to evangelistic, conventional and restrained in worship as opposed to emotional and spontaneous, ritualist and élitist in religious expression as opposed to mass participatory. In each of the above pairs, the first of the paired modes tends to be associated with religious groups consisting of upper- and middle-class members, and the second with lower-class members. (Goodall, 1970.) For example, to take an extreme, contrast the staid Episcopalian congregations of the urban upper-middle-class United States to the snake-handling religious ecstasy of congregations of rural working-class people in Tennessee. In a study of 27 "churches" in Lethbridge, Alberta, a curvilinear pattern of religious-class behaviour was discovered. The spontaneity of lower-class sects contrasted to the formal proceedings of lower-middle-class churches, to the relative informality of middle-class church behaviour, to the semi-formality of upper-middle and upper-class churches. (Goodall, 1970.)

In Canada evidence suggests that religious organizations clearly stratify by class composition. The Anglican, Presbyterian, and United Churches are characteristically upper class in membership, as are Jewish congregations. Other Protestant denominations and the Roman Catholic Church are characteristically lower class in membership. (Teevan, Jr. and Jackson, 1972.)

Table 4-7

Class composition of major religious denominations in the U.S.A.

Religion	Rank
Jewish	1
Episcopalian	2
Congregationalist	3
Presbyterian	4
Methodist	5
Catholic	6
Lutheran	7
Baptist	8

Source: Gockel "Income and Religious Affiliation: A Regression Analysis", *American Journal of Sociology* 74 (1969) Table 1.

In the United States the rank order of religious denominations by family income, occupational level, and education, is summarized in Table 4-7.

When compared with Canadian data, the hierarchy of denominations is remarkably similar, as for example, in the top rank of the Jewish and Anglican (Episcopalian), and the low standing of the Roman Catholic Church. Based on a Toronto sample, Teevan and Jackson examined the mean income, education, and occupational standing of the heads of families attending various denominations. They report that Jews, Anglicans, United Church, and Presbyterians are all well above the mean levels, while the Lutherans, Baptists, Roman Catholics, and Greek Orthodox, are below the average levels. (Teevan Jr. and Jackson, 1972: 5.)

Table 4-8

Mean values of income, education, and occupational level, by religious denomination male household heads, Toronto, 1968

Denomination	Income (N)	Education (N)	Occupational (N) Level*
Jewish	$10778 (54)	12.1 (61)	29.3 (63)
Anglican	8873 (307)	11.4 (327)	39.2 (336)
United Church	8793 (334)	11.6 (341)	39.0 (354)
Presbyterian	8284 (102)	11.3 (112)	41.1 (115)
Lutheran	7921 (57)	11.0 (59)	40.8 (63)
Baptist	7622 (37)	10.7 (40)	39.6 (41)
Roman Catholic	6928 (423)	9.3 (467)	53.6 (484)
Greek Orthodox	5678 (45)	8.5 (47)	56.5 (49)
TOTAL	8100 (1359)	10.7 (1454)	43.9 (1505)

Source: Teevan Jr. and Jackson, 1972.
Lower scores are for higher status occupation.

Consistent with these findings, Allingham reports that in Ontario the Anglican Church consists of relatively homogenously high-economic-status persons. The United, Presbyterian, and Baptist Churches are less homogeneous in class standing of members, although still tending to consist of relatively high-status persons employed in government and corporate administration, whom he termed the "bureaucratic élite". (Allingham, 1962.) Over all, in rank order of members' status, Allingham listed the Anglican, Jewish, Presbyterian, Greek Orthodox, Baptist, United Church, and Roman Catholic church. (Allingham, 1962.) These findings correspond with the 1968 Toronto study of Teeven and Jackson, with the exception of the United Church, which the Toronto researchers found, as in the United States, to rank in the top levels.

It would be difficult to attribute "success" or class membership to religious belief or membership in any clear-cut casual sense. But it is the case that certain religions in Canada are associated with certain ethnic groups and social classes and therefore, insofar as class standing is inherited, so too is religious membership. There are exceptions among persons active in religious activities, as evidenced in findings suggesting that persons enjoying upward social mobility will associate themselves with the appropriately upper-status denominations. (Teevan Jr. and Jackson, 1972.) However, generally the point is that there exists a hierarchy of church rank in Canada, congruent with the class structure of Canadian society.

What is more important is that the ideology of the several religions will reinforce existing class attitudes, behaviour, and structure. Of particular import, this includes political behaviour and social change. Election data show that persons of Protestant affiliation will tend to vote for the Progressive Conservative Party, a reflection of class and ethnic membership. On the other hand, Jews and Roman Catholics will tend to vote for the Liberal Party. (Alford, 1963: 1965.) These data lump together varying denominations as Protestant, and are confounded with regional and ethnic effects, but there is some evidence to suggest that these patterns of voting by religion persist even when the effects of ethnicity and social class are controlled. (Anderson, 1964.) This would mean that religious affiliation may act to over-ride class economic interests.

Table 4-9

Party support by religion, 1962, in pre-election poll

	Religion				
Party	Protestant	% Jewish	Catholic	Other*	Total
P.C.	47	19	24	27	36
Liberal	29	58	49	17	38
N.D.P.	13	23	8	27	12
Socred	11	—	19	29	14
100% =	(1187)	(47)	(915)	(41)	(2190)

*"Other" includes those not answering the question on religion.

Source: Alford, 1964: 214.

We have seen that aggregating the Protestant religious denominations suggests a Protestant conservatism. However, we may recall from previous discussion that this is not altogether true. Methodists and United Church members were instrumental in organizing and supporting the C.C.F., for example. Not only was J.S. Woodsworth a minister, as we previously noted, but T.C. Douglas, who succeeded to the leadership of the party and the Premier's office in Saskatchewan, later national leader, is a Baptist minister. Stanley Knowles, long returned to the House of Commons from North Winnipeg, is a United Church minister. (Crysdale and Beattie, 1973: 282.) In the contiguous tradition of rural protest and third party formation, William Aberhardt was a Baptist minister.

In contrast, the Anglican Church and the Roman Catholic Church have been associated with opposition to the C.C.F./N.D.P. The Anglican Church in Canada has been the church of the upper-middle and upper classes of British origin and thereby has, in its opposition, been acting class consistently. The Roman Catholic Church, the affiliation of French Canadians and lower-status immigrants, has not been so class consistent in its opposition to anything smacking of socialism or "Godless" communism. But in Quebec the Roman Catholic Church clergy of superior rank were historically part of the economic and political establishment, as Rioux noted (Rioux, 1971), and closely allied with the provincial Union Nationale Party. Part of the "middle class revolt" in Quebec that saw Jean Lesage's Liberal Party turn out the Union Nationale was also anti-church, as is the present Parti Québecois support. In addition, the Roman Catholic Church has tended to be antiunion; Clark states that it was the church influence upon French-Canadian workers in northern Quebec and Ontario company towns that prevented the formation of labour unions in opposition to company influence, as we noted in Chapter Two. (Clark, 1971.)

Despite the widely assumed notion that religion is becoming obsolete in our secular society, it is in fact the case that religious institutions continue to play an important role in socializing and influencing Canadians. One need not be a regular or frequent adult attender of a church, nor even attend church at all as an adult, to have learned in childhood ideological outlooks that persist in influencing behaviour. At times these influences are to the detriment of class interests, but in other instances, as we have seen, actively promote class awareness and interests.

Conclusions

Previously we had considered the structure of class stratification in Canada, and the opportunities for mobility. But class means more than differences in wealth or occupational choice. There are real differences in the benefits that we might consider fundamental to human existence, as well as the more obvious differences in the consumption of luxury items. The Canadian welfare state does secure basic sustenance, clothing, shelter, and health care for Canadians, but these benefits are by no means uniformly available. Rather, they are systematically associated in quantity and in quality with urbanized middle- and upper-class existence. The class structure thereby enforces a discrimination in basic human benefits.

Class-related discrimination is also reflected in the nature of criminal deviance and the nature of law enforcement. Lower-class deviance is necessarily conspicuous, and often violent. There are not the opportunities for hidden theft that are available to the middle-class person. In addition, police activity tends to concentrate upon lower-class persons, in part because of the aggressive public nature of criminal deviance by lower-class persons, but also because lower-class persons are vulnerable and unlikely to be able to avoid prosecution.

Ironically, as a function of environmental experience and expectations, lower-class persons assume that they will be the objects of harassment and violence, but also are less tolerant than are middle-class persons of moderate punishment and due process. This lower-class intolerance has been characterized as a working-class authoritarianism and has been taken in part to account for lower-class political conservatism in the sense of support for right-wing parties.

The nature of political action is of crucial import, for class interests and their realization are to be found in political action. Conservative support seems contrary to lower-class economic interests and a manifestation of false consciousness. Such non-interest-oriented behaviour seems also related to religious ideology. Some denominations, such as the Roman Catholic, have consistently espoused conservative support and have actively discouraged socialist sympathy on the part of members, while the Anglicans have been class consistent in their conservative inclinations. In contrast, other denominations, such as the Methodist, seem to have articulated a class awareness and responsibility inclined to socialist support.

The ideological input of religion, and of immigrants committed to ideological philosophies, has had considerable impact upon the development of protest and its character in Canada. Protest has related to the regional expression of class interests. Whether socialist or non-socialist, such protest movements as have developed are class-related, in the sense of recognition of a situation of shared relative deprivation, and collective action to the end of rectifying that situation.

To a considerable extent the political protest and opposition have been agrarian, but we are of the view that, in the context of Canadian regional relations, such agrarian action is consistent with class interests and action. In an industrialized society, the large or corporate agriculturalists aside, the farmer, though an owner, is in an economic position akin to that of the industrial worker, and with perhaps less security. Rural interests are thus expressed in agricultural unions, co-operatives, and third-party support, as labour has expressed its interests in labour-union organization. The opposition of interests between corporate industrial capitalists and farmer is essentially the same as that between industrial owners and financiers and the blue-collar or white-collar worker. This is especially a volatile incompatibility, as the agrarian interests are vested in a region's subordination to the metropolitan influence of industrialized Ontario. Class-based social action seeking the alteration of this dominance is the subject of our concluding chapter.

5

CLASS CONFLICT AND PROSPECTS FOR CHANGE

Class and Change

In the 19th century Karl Marx and Frederick Engels argued that the interests of capitalists and those of workers were inherently contradictory. Inevitably, class conflict would become overt, and the revolutionary victory of the workers would come to pass. For Marx and Engels the concept of class was not just a description of the structure of economic control, but more important it was the key to a theory of social change. The working class, as a collectivity conscious of its relations to the property ownership of the capitalists, was to be the vehicle of societal progress, ultimately realizing full equality of condition in a communist society.

Although Marx offered no time frame within which the revolution would occur, many observers have delighted in noting the apparent failure of Marxist predictions. Rather than become more impoverished, workers have shared in industrial prosperity to an extent Marx failed to anticipate, while *lumpenproletariat* have been extended considerable welfare privileges. Rather than a class polarization, a "new" class of white-collar employees and professionals has developed and served to insulate the lower class from the upper class. Rather than fewer and fewer capitalists controlling the means of production, ownership has been dispersed in corporate structures and their shareholders and managers.

These features of modern capitalist societies are factual enough; it is their interpretation that is open to debate. The possibility of class action persists insofar as there persists a basic opposition of interest between owners and workers. The working class may share in industrial benefits to some degree, but, especially recalling the concept of relative deprivation, they do not share to the point of satisfaction, let alone equity. The unemployed may be supported by the state, using funds collected from wage-workers, but they are not thereby somehow rendered full and equal participants in society. The middle class may have acquired some measure of job security and consumer ability, but they have not gained any greater control over the economy. Formal ownership may have largely passed from individuals to corporations, but the ownership is not any less concentrated. Rather it is more concentrated, given the size of modern corporations with the effective ownership vested in one or a few individuals possessing blocs of shares. Changes in class affluence have not altered the fundamental relations of production and control in Western societies such as Canada's. It is not a matter of rescuing Marxist theory, but of recognizing the continued salience of his descriptions, however much he may have failed to anticipate the massive potentials of industrial societies to produce and distribute wealth and to defer and control class opposition. However, whether the opposition of interests of which Marx spoke and which does obtain in altered form in Canada will result in overt conflict and significant change is far more open to question.

In Western societies, and in Canada in particular, there obviously has always been class conflict, for example, as manifested in strike activities. And increasingly, the organization of employees and resort to strike is an aspect of white-collar and professional employees as well as of manual workers, perhaps suggesting the class polarization that Marx anticipated. In this chapter, concentrating in large part upon the relationships of organized labour to employer and government, we shall consider the Canadian experience of class conflict, and the prospect for action that might alter the Canadian stratification system.

The Working Class and Conflict in Canada

Much of our earlier discussion has stressed the stability of social stratification in Canada and the apparent absence of any non-rural class consciousness. Yet, Canadian history is replete with instances of overt conflict among social classes, conflict indicative of a consciousness and effective in generating such a consciousness. Often class awareness and conflict have been expressed simply as a reciprocal hostility, as in the attitudes and comments of members of the lower and upper classes, with the middle class characteristically echoing upper-class sentiment. Thus, the lower-class distrust and resentment of welfare agents, for example, and the middle- and upper-class declarations of their tax-paying virtue, are indicative of widely shared antagonisms. Or, similarly indicative of some awareness, though "false consciousness" as far as a Marxist would be concerned, are the non-unionized Canadians' suspicion of unions, and the inclination to blame labour organizations not only for disruptions in services, but for international economic trends such as inflation.

In the Canadian experience, class hostility was most explicit during the early phases of unionization, especially the years immediately preceeding World War I, through the war years, and into the depression of the 1930s. During the depression, for example, Canadians were certainly made aware of differential privilege, as the prosperous who survived the economic disaster regarded the indigent with disdain, who in turn reciprocated with bitterness and hostility. Gray relates many such examples, as in the case of a group of relief-workers on a make-work project in Winnipeg being harassed by an indignant citizen, furious over this disposition of his tax money on "lazy bums". In turn the "bums", persons who had lost their jobs, responded with threats of violence. (Gray, 1966: 45.) But often, as we shall go on to consider, the violence was more than a threat, but a realization.

Additionally, the conflict of classes has been linked to ethnic bias in Canadian history. In 1918, for example, riots in Quebec City were a feature of French-Canadian lower-class opposition to military conscription. (McNaught, 1970: 81.) The internment of Japanese Canadians on the west coast during World War II was an instance of the authorities acting against an entire ethnic group. The current Indian protests, expressed in blockading highways in British Columbia, occupying a park in Kenora, Ontario, or the march to Ottawa that climaxed in the violent confrontation on Parliament Hill between Indians and the R.C.M.P., are class-related conflicts.

There is a long tradition of such ethnic-class distinction and conflict, as long as the history of contact among Indians, Europeans, Euro-Canadians, Anglo-Canadians, and non-Anglo immigrants in Canada. In World War I the invocation of the War Measures Act led to several thousand arrests and summary deportations of immigrant workers who failed to satisfy the Anglo-Canadian definition of loyalty. (Brown and Brown, 1973: 36.) Similarly, in the depression the government resorted to arrest and deportation of "aliens" as one means of alleviating the number of unemployed. As Gray recalls:

> . . . I came to appreciate for the first time the tremendous advantage it was to be a Canadian Anglo-Saxon in Winnipeg. And as time passed, the advantage widened when, as if racial intolerance was not enough, a new terror for the New Canadians began to stalk the land in the form of Immigration Officers with deportation orders in their hands. In 1931 the Communist Party was outlawed and the party leaders were arrested and sent to jail under the notorious Section 98 of the Criminal Code. Other aliens who were suspected of Commuunist activity were arrested at night and rushed secretly to Halifax for deportation.
>
> (Gray, 1966: 131)

Such actions, and the confrontation of ethnic minorities including Indians with government, are aspects of class in Canada and are explicit manifestations of conflict between the privileged upper or ruling class in Canada and lower-class persons in Canada's "ethnic mosaic". Usually, thus far the middle class as a collectivity has "opted out", although middle-class individuals have been crucial in their participation and organization of opposition actions. The major foci of the tradition of conflict have been labour and agrarian action. We have discussed agrarian protest in Chapter Four, and require only a few additional remarks as prelude to a brief description of related conflict involving the industrial worker as well as the rural worker. We will note three major occasions of class confrontation in Canadian society: the Winnipeg General Strike of 1919; the "On to Ottawa Trek" of 1935; and the Saskatchewan Doctors' Strike of 1962.

Farm Protest Politics

When we looked at the pattern of agrarian protest and third-party support in Canada, we found it concentrated in the Canadian West. Elsewhere Quebec farmers have perceived themselves to be in fundamental disharmony with urban Canada. In 1974 farmers across the nation protested prices, most dramatically in Quebec, where there were several instances of calves being slaughtered and buried.

Donald Creighton, a conservative Canadian historian, has suggested that radical political action in Canada has been a fluctuation, though not a synthesis, of labour and agrarian radicalism. (Creighton, 1972: 160.) Thus in the wake of labour action and the Winnipeg General Strike emerged the agrarian Progressive Party, which was to provide the setting for the emergence of a prairie socialism, and the Co-operative Commonwealth Federation (CCF). The Progressive Party was a rural party, expressing the interests and frustrations of people in the Prairies and in Ontario who perceived themselves lacking in influence and their share of national resources. W.L. Morton views prairie support for the Progressives as a manifestation of protest against the colonial status of the West in relation to eastern business interests. (Morton, 1950: 164-65.)

The Prairies, locus of most radical farm politics, have also been the source of considerable labour-union radicalism. The two have underlined regional cleavage in Canada.

Labour Protest Politics

In Canada the history of labour-union organization and activities has been the most explicit example of class conflict. We find lower-class worker pitted against upper-middle and upper-class manager and employer. Strikes have been the direct expression of class conflict. Today, when we are well past the initial phases of labour-union organization, we take for granted that strikes are pacific withdrawals of service, with perhaps only an occasional picket-line skirmish. Today large-scale labour violence, such as at the James Bay Hydro project, with its apparent organized resort to violence, seems extraordinary. However, similar violence was once routine in North America, with strikers on the one side, and the police and strike-breakers hired by employers on the other. For example, the Royal Canadian (Northwest) Mounted Police were frequently brought in to break up strikes, particularly in the Canadian West around World War I. (Brown and Brown, 1973: 38-45.) In this regard, it is interesting to note the argument that the Winnipeg General Strike may have saved the Royal Northwest Mounted Police from disbandment, for it established an important strike-breaking role for them. (Brown and Brown, 1973: 45.)

The latter quarter of the 19th century and the years prior to World War I were conflict-filled years in class relations in Canada. The years 1876 to 1914 saw troops called out 33 times to control and put down strikes in Ontario, Quebec, and the Maritimes. (McNaught, 1970: 80.) After the war, labour action intensified as the veterans returned. In 1914 trade-union membership in Canada numbered 166 000. By 1919 membership was approximately 378 000. (Creighton, 1972: 158.) In this period the overt conflict of classes was unmistakable. The year 1919 saw 336 strikes and lockouts, involving 150 000 workers. (Creighton, 1972: 159.)

During this period a marked difference between western and eastern labour became apparent, in no small part attributable to European settlement in the West and the immigration of British settlers with socialist and labour-union experience, as we noted in describing the development of the C.C.F. Robin states that the West was far more radical than the East. (Robin, 1968: 160.) S.D. Clark suggests that both labour and agrarian protest in the West were manifestations of western Canadian opposition to "eastern dominance". (Clark, 1950: vii; Creighton, 1972: 159.) The cleavage became especially apparent in 1918, at the Trades and Labour Congress meeting in Quebec City. (Robin, 1968: 160.) At this time, the western inclination for political education of workers and political action surfaced as a minority view; eventually two western socialists were ousted as officers, and a new congress president was elected. The new president, Tom Moore, was a personal friend of the American unionist, Samuel Gompers. (Robin, 1968: 160-162.) This highlighted a persisting split in the character of Canadian labour; eastern labour organizations have been internationalist — that is, affiliated with American unions — while western unions have often been stubbornly nationalist, even when formally affiliated with American-based unions.

In the West, at the Western Labour Conference held in Calgary in 1919, the notion of One Big Union (OBU) grew up, amidst statements of support for "Russian Bolsheviks". (Robin, 1968: 175; Penner, 1973: xiii.) The concept of the OBU was dear to the socialists, who reasoned that it would be a means to class consciousness, and the strike would be the means of political action. (Robin, 1968: 175-176.) The OBU was never to be realized; nor was there ever a consensus about the concept, even in the West. (Robin, 1968: 177.) But it set the mood for events in Winnipeg in 1919.

Winnipeg was a centre of strong support for the OBU concept and generally the centre of labour protest in Canada. (Robin, 1968: 168, 191-192.) One of the causes of protest was an Order in Council passed by the federal government on October 11, 1918, restricting speech, association, publications, and above all, the right to strike. (Robin, 1968: 166.).

Winnipeg, 1919, and After

The Winnipeg General Strike began on May 15, 1919, and lasted until June 25. (Penner, 1973: xxv-xxvii.) It featured labour on the one side and the Winnipeg Citizens Committee, consisting of businessmen and professionals, on the other. Special police, the R.C.M.P., and the regular army ultimately confronted the strikers in the streets of Winnipeg.

The upper class perceived the situation to be a challenge to authority, a presage of revolution. The workers and labour leaders saw it as a matter of demanding higher wages, and collective bargaining as a means to realizing such demands. There is little doubt that neither side really understood the other, an apt illustration of the varying perceptions and ideologies of social classes. The political authorities, such as Mayor Gray, seemed to be bewildered by events, which seemed to be running out of control, obliging resort to force. The newspapers were consistently opposed to the strikers, characterizing them as aliens and communists. On the other hand, to the strikers the authorities were selfish and ruthless exploiters. In May the Citizens Committee started to publish *The Winnipeg Citizen*, wherein strikers were portrayed as agents of lawlessness and foreign revolution. For example, appearing in *The Winnipeg Citizen* were statements of the following sort:

> Lawlessness and disorder are rampant throughout the city all day and every day. Men and women are wantonly assaulted on the streets.
>
> (Balawyder, 1967: 1)

> "The citizens of Winnipeg have been fighting . . . .against a determined effort to establish Bolshevism and the rule of the Soviet here and then to expand it all over the Dominion. . . ."
>
> (Balawyder, 1967: 19)

To the present day, establishment historians persist in viewing the strike as a violent and deplorable aberration. Labour is held accountable, rather than their class opponents, or the mounted and armed police who charged the strikers on "Bloody Saturday". For example, Donald Creighton's acclaimed history of Canada's first century devotes one page to the strike, and refers to it as the "Winnipeg riot". (Creighton, 1972: 60.)

The strike was called in sympathy with construction and metal trades workers who were striking for an eight-hour day. (Balawyder, 1967: 1-3.) At its peak, the strikers effectively withdrew all services, from transportation, milk and bread deliveries, postal deliveries, to firemen, telegraphers, and civic employees including policemen. (Balawyder, 1967; Penner, 1973.) On the first day, 27 000 workers were out. (Balawyder, 1967: 3.) At its peak, there were 35 000 strikers in a population of 175 000, where, at day one of the strike, the Trades and Labour Council membership numbered only 12 000. (Penner, 1973: x.)

Insofar as the unions were concerned, the strike consisted not of demonstrations and "lawlessness" but of simple withdrawal of services. However, an additional ingredient in the situation consisted of servicemen returned from the war. Numerous parades were organized by the soldiers caught in unemployment on their return. On June 21 one such parade was attacked by armed special police, mounted police, and members of the regular army, in the effective climax of the strike. One marcher was killed and many injured.[1] (Penner, 1973: x.)

From the onset the federal government viewed the strike as dangerous. There was some real threat of its spreading across the country, with sympathetic activity in Toronto and Vancouver in particular. (Balawyder, 1967: 24-25.) Thus, Winnipeg civic authorities and the federal government were in perfect agreement in their opposition to the strikers. Arthur Meighen, who would later become Prime Minister of Canada, was the principle agent of the federal government, as acting Minister of Justice in the Borden government. Meighen shared the ruling class ideological beliefs and had close relationships to the Winnipeg business community, the heart of the Citizens Committee. (Penner, 1973: xviii.)

With civic and federal authorities co-ordinating their responses, the governments acted to confront rather than negotiate with the strikers. On May 26, the Winnipeg Citizens Committee voted to fire all civic employees who went out on strike. On June 5 the federal government passed an amendment to the Immigration Act, allowing the deportation of British-born immigrants, so that the government would arrest and be rid of some of the leaders of the strike. (Robin, 1968: 181.) On June 9, all but 16 members of the Winnipeg police force were fired for failing to sign an anti-strike promise, an action leading to the formation of the special police force on June 10. (Balawyder, 1967: x.) June 17 saw the arrest by federal authorities of 12 strike leaders, including J.S. Woodsworth. (Balawyder, 1967: 4.) Then, after the violent confronta-

[1]Balawyder reports two killed, 30 injured. (1967: 5)

tion of June 21, soldiers and police patrolled the streets of the city, fully armed with pistols and machine guns. The police charge of June 21 effectively destroyed support for the strike, and on June 25 it ended. (Balawyder, 1967: 5.)

The labour radicalism of the West, the activities and strategies of the socialists, the decision to form the One Big Union were the background events of the strike. That it was a characteristic western event is evidenced by the fact that most of the international unions, which as we have noted were strongest in eastern Canada, opposed the strike. (Robin, 1968: 184.) The autonomous unions of the West were strongly influenced by British socialist officers, who in turn were influential in the strike. (Penner, 1973: xix.) For reasons of immigration and background, and because of the circumstances of western Canada and its colonial-like relationship to eastern Canada, the manifestation of class consciousness and class conflict, urban and agrarian, were viable in the West to an extent not true of the East.

In the years after the strike, labour organization in Canada grew, although it did not resort to dramatic confrontation like that of 1919. Creighton states that the strike marked the deflation of radical labour politics. (Creighton, 1972: 60.) But through the 1920s Canadian labour was active and aggressive. In terms of Canadian autonomy, Abella suggests that up to and peaking in 1935, Canadian unions were at their strongest, with about one half the union membership in independent Canadian unions. In 1921 the Canadian and Catholic Confederation of Labour was founded, explicitly nationalist and anti-American. In 1927 the All Canadian Congress of Labour was founded and was characteristically nationalist through the 1930s. In 1930 the radical Workers' Unity League came into being, to a large degree under communist control. (Abella, 1973: 2-3.) With the exception of the Catholic Federation, largely active in Quebec, the Communist Party of Canada was active in union leadership, especially in the Workers' Unity League.

Abella notes that the Communist Party was instrumental in the destruction of independent Canadian union activity in that in 1935 they ordered the disbandment of the Workers' Unity League in favour of affiliation with the Trades and Labour Congress, an affiliate of the American Federation of Labour. The communist objective was a united labour front. (Abella, 1973:3.) After 1935 American affiliates came to dominate. In large part, in addition to the Communist Party decision, this was due to the actions of Ontario labour organizers rather than the Americans themselves. (Abella, 1973: 2; 5; 216.) The model of the American unions and their apparent successes proved too attractive, though as Abella notes it is questionable whether they ever played more than a role of moral support in aid of Canadian workers; certainly they never aided financially, for in fact Canadian dues went south to a greater degree than financial aid came north. (Abella, 1973.) Despite

American union affiliation, one unique feature of the Canadian unions persisted: a flirtation with socialism and eventually a socialist party, the C.C.F.-N.D.P. Horowitz suggests that even the Trades and Labour Congress never repudiated socialism in the unequivocal manner of the American unions. (Horowitz, 1968: 58.) But affiliation with American unions was effectively to prevent formal explicit labour affiliation with the yet to emerge C.C.F.-N.D.P. (Horowitz, 1968: 235.)

The year 1936 marked the entry of the Congress of Industrial Organization (C.I.O.) to Canada, at the instigation of Ontario Labour leaders. (Abella, 1973: 210.) In 1937 the C.I.O. was organizing steel workers in Nova Scotia, and also found itself in a dramatic confrontation in Oshawa, Ontario. (Abella, 1973: 5; 21-22.) The Oshawa strike against General Motors by the United Auto Workers established the C.I.O. as a powerful labour organization in Canada. (Abella, 1973: 21-22.)

From this period, only in western Canada did marked nationalist labour sentiment crop up, especially in British Columbia unions, where periodically movements to secede from American-based unions would occur. (Abella, 1973: 111-138.) Also, western labour radicalism would live on even within the Canadian Congress of Labour, the result of a 1939 merger of the C.I.O. and the All Canadian Congress of Labour; the latter included remnants of the One Big Union movement (Abella, 1973: 44), a dream that was finally to collapse during the Great Depression.

Depression and the On to Ottawa Trek

The depression set the stage for a dramatic confrontation between workers and authorities. Through the decade of the thirties incidents were numerous between the unemployed and the police. Particularly, at this time, the railroad police of the Canadian Pacific Railway established a reputation for viciousness among the unemployed "riding the rails".

The specific policy of the depression that elicited both working-class and middle-class bitterness related to the creation of the relief work camps. On October 8, 1932, the work camps were created by Order in Council of the federal government. (Horowitz, 1973: viii.) They were set up and administered by the federal authorities, and by 1934 they contained 25 000 young men. After four years of operation 115 000 men had occupied the camps at one time or another. (Gray, 1967: 147.)

The camps were the objects of middle- and upper-class abuse because they were make-work projects, and thereby a waste of public funds. Yet they were created not only to occupy the unemployed and remove them from urban centres, but also to satisfy middle-class values, in that they did require labour rather than welfare on the simple basis of need. For the unemployed workers, they were the supreme insult and degradation. Existing in isolation, spawning boredom, with a reservation-like system of administration wherein no organizations were permitted, no grievance procedures allowed the inhabitants, and with wages of 20 cents a day, the bitterness was inevitable. (Gray, 1967: 147-148.)

On April 4, 1935, 1500 relief camp workers moved into Vancouver in order to protest their situation and seek some change in government policy. (Hoar, 1973: ix.) The work camps had been the sites of active propagandizing and organizing by the Communist Party of Canada, and by the time of the Vancouver assembly, the workers not only were in a mood for action, but had leaders ready and able to promote it. (Gray, 1967: 145.) But in no sense was it a communist movement; it was a genuine act of disillusioned people who wished to work. With assistance from supporters such as the Liberal mayor of Vancouver, who sponsored a tag day netting $6 000, a march was organized, with Ottawa the objective. (Gray, 1967: 150.)

The marchers left Vancouver on June 3 and June 4, 1935, about 1 000 strong. (Gray, 1967: 151.) It now seems that early on the federal government determined to stop the march, and Regina was the logical place because of the concentration of Royal Canadian Mounted Police in that city. On June 14 the marchers arrived in Regina, now about 2 000 in number. (Gray, 1967: 152.) Then they were ordered to halt by the government, and talks were arranged.

The talks proved to be utterly fruitless. As Gray reports, "It degenerated into a shouting match between the Prime Minister and Arthur Evans, the strike leader. Mr. Bennett called Evans a thief, and Evans called the Prime Minister a liar." (Gray, 1967: 155.) On July 2 a mass rally attended by an estimated 3500 to 4500 marchers and on-lookers was held in Market Square in Regina. (Gray; 1963: 158.) The city police and the R.C.M.P. were ordered in, and at their appearance in force the crowd panicked. Fighting developed, barricades were erected, and spectators, strikers, and police were injured. It lasted three hours and concluded with a dead policeman, several more injured, about six civilians with bullet wounds, and about 80 people under arrest. (Gray, 1967: 159.)

The leaders were in jail and the trek was effectively broken. By July 5, the strikers had dispersed. (Hoar, 1973; xv-xviii.) At about the same time, other protesters in Winnipeg dispersed, just avoiding a similar police-striker confrontation. (Gray, 1967: 157-159.) Two weeks later some trekkers were attempting to carry on, and about 250 made it on foot to Kenora after their buses were stopped at the Manitoba-Ontario border by the Ontario Provincial Police. After three days these trekkers gave up and returned to Winnipeg. (Gray, 1967: 160.)

The specific clash in Regina would probably today be called a "police riot", for it resulted from police action, acting on government orders. As in the Winnipeg General Strike, the entire trek was characterized by a class polarization of sentiment. James Gray, who covered the events as a reporter for *Winnipeg Free Press*, states that the trekkers did have sympathetic treatment from the press and were generally met with favour by the public, until the shouting match between Bennett and Evans. (Gray, 1967; 151-152; 155.) But even so, it seems fairer to say that both sides were locked into extreme views of each other; the government was callous and oppressive and the workers were communists. (Hoar, 1973: ix.)

The Dominion Day battle in Regina was merely the conspicuous event in a prolonged situation of class conflict. Protests against the relief programs had been occurring elsewhere before 1935, as in Vancouver in 1931 and Winnipeg in 1934. Once again, western Canada was the setting for the more radical political action.

The Second World War marked the end of the depression and of mass radical labour politics. Certainly the bitter memories lived on, not least among unemployed Canadians who found a secure income only in the armed forces. We recall the remark of one Canadian veteran, who in the 1970s summed up his analysis of the situation in the sentiment that, "Hitler was the one who got me a job!" Afterwards came the post-war industrial boom in North America. Canada in particular enjoyed a brief major-power status and a flurry of Canadian-controlled industry. Wages were high and welfare policies were extended to all classes. Yet even the gradual introduction of welfare security programs of the sort taken for granted in 1974 were occasions of class conflict. The most dramatic example also occured in western Canada.

The Doctors' Strike

Our third example of class conflict involved the middle class as the strikers. In July 1966, medical doctors in Saskatchewan commenced what would become a 23-day withdrawal of services, in protest against the Saskatchewan government's comprehensive health care insurance program. The C.C.F. government, abiding by its campaign promises, was determined to implement medical insurance to protect people against the economic fluctuations of the Saskatchewan economy. They were contested by the doctors, who were determined to preserve their "*laissez-faire* definition of medical practice", or services for purchase. (Badgley and Wolfe, 1967: 5.) It became in large part a rural-urban conflict between the farm population and the doctors and their urban supporters. Fifty-four per cent of Saskatchewan physicians practised in Regina and Saskatoon, where only 22 per cent of the population lived. (Badgley and Wolfe, 1973: 28.)

The medical insurance legislation became the target of a very expensive campaign, with a Keep Our Doctors Committee in the vanguard. The K.O.D. consisted of non-C.C.F. politicians, druggists, dentists, businessmen, and some clergy, with ties to the provincial Liberal Party. (Badgley and Wolfe, 1973: 52.) The K.O.D. publicity equated medical insurance with "Marxism and Communism". (Badgley and Wolfe, 1973: 31.) To mount the campaign, aside from citizen donations, there was a $100 levy from all doctors in the province, plus $35 000 from the Canadian Medical Association. (Badgely and Wolfe, 1973: 74.)

In oppostion to the K.O.D. were the government, trade unions, the farmers' union, and the co-op organizations. In 1961 a survey of small communities showed that 63 per cent of the population favoured health care, but less than half (46 per cent) of the upper class, as opposed to 70 per cent of the lower class, were in favour. (Badgely and Wolfe, 1973: 74.) Thus the conflict did polarize by class, and the opposition publicity in the media was almost total. Except for the Canadian Broadcasting Corporation, the media supported the K.O.D. (Badgely and Wolfe, 1973: 74.)

Ultimately, of course, the doctors capitulated, in no small part because the government, rather than compromising, resorted to importing doctors from the United Kingdom. But around this one issue the potential of class conflict again crystalized in one region of Canadian society.

The Examples in Context

The three examples of class conflict we have related may be taken in two ways. One might simply view them as interesting aberrations in the evolution of Canadian society and therefore not of continuing relevance. Or, as we suggest, one may view them as symptomatic of and the product of fundamental stratification in Canada. Where the conflict among classes may usually remain subdued and invisible, these three incidents were occasions in which the opposition of classes in Canada broke through. And they illustrate the manner in which social class in Canada is intimately inter-related with regional and ethnic differences, underlining the Anglo-eastern-Canadian dominant status within Canadian society. The three examples are probably the best known and documented in Canadian history, but they are not the only instances of conflict among classes. Others have been as violent. In the 1920s, for example, labour-management violence occured in Cape Breton Island, Nova Scotia, involving attempts to prevent unionization. Similarly, troops were used to put down strike action by steel workers in Sydney. In Estevan, Saskatchewan, September 1931 saw a miners' strike when their union was not recognized; ultimately, the R.C.M.P. again acted as strike-breakers and the strike was broken, with two dead. Racial-class violence was a feature of the computer destruction at Sir George Williams University in Montreal in 1969. And, among other violent strikes, the Murray Hill taxi strike in Montreal resulted in a death. The labour violence in 1974 at the James Bay Hydroelectric Development in northern Quebec is another instance, one that seems to involve not only labour and owners, but also a conflict between a Quebec union and an international union — not insignificant given the previously remarked less radical role of American-based unions in Canada. Lastly, we cannot fail to note that Quebec separatism is a class movement as well as an ethnic movement, one in which the new middle class of post-war Quebec has in some considerable degree committed itself to radical action, with the end both independence and socialism.

If such conflict is not abnormal but a continuing feature of Canadian society, deriving from the class distinctions that exist in Canada, then the prospects of change in aid of a non-violent and genuinely egalitarian or minimally stratified society must concern us.

Class Conflict and Welfare Politics

Organized Labour

If the number of strikes, and their duration, during 1973 and 1974 are taken as indicators, Canada is now experiencing an increased aggressiveness in labour-union activity. In large part, the increased labour demands are a response to inflation and relate to a pursuit of immediate or short-term economic advantage, rather than any drive for basic change in social organization. In such two-party economic bargaining, unions are relatively successful in terms of gaining wage concessions. But when interested at all in influencing government policies, unions have not been effective in Canada. Presthus has reported that, although many elected representatives in Canada believe unions to be effective pressure groups, an analysis of actual government decisions shows that in fact it is professional and business interests that are dominantly effective in influencing decision outcomes. (Presthus, 1974: 207.) The union influence seems great only at the point of specific bargaining confrontation. Unlike previous instances of conflict in Canada, labour actions have become conventionalized or institutionalized, with affluence and general acceptance and legitimation of collective bargaining. Class conflict has not disappeared but, rather than becoming extreme, it has and likely will continue to be pacified. Thereby it will be increasingly less likely to promote significant structural change.

The organized economic bargaining has increasingly extended to white-collar workers and professionals. Teachers' unions, professors' unions on several Canadian campuses, and the large Public Service Alliance of Canada are examples of the unionization and, perhaps, despite their affluence, the mobilization of the hitherto placid middle class. What is absent in such action, however, is any ideological loading or sentiment that differs from hitherto prevailing "centre" attitudes of middle-class Canadians. Insofar as people are becoming increasingly engaged in confrontation with employers, such confrontation is purely out of collective or shared short-term interest, and not interest in a fundamental improvement in class economic situation or ideological conviction of an egalitarian sort.

The extent to which such pedestrian activities become radicalized will be a function of government and employer response and the occurrence or not of any major economic crisis. Given economic disruption, middle-class persons have educational and organizational skills that are translatable into effective opposition politics. But that opposition is as apt to be conservative, as in the Saskatchewan doctors' strike, as it is to be socialist, as in Quebec separatism. A crucial variable will be perceived relative deprivation; economic jeopardy could realize the class polarization Marxists anticipated so long ago. Conceivably massive inflation could precipitate a middle-class "revolution" — again, not necessarily a left-wing revolution — involving skilled workers and professionals. The situation of the pre-war German Weimar Republic resembles such a hypothetical situation.

For many years some social theorists have been predicting the development of white-collar or middle-class consciousness, meaning a recognition of economic affinity to other workers and opposition to owners. (Mills, 1951; Lockwood, 1958.) But there is a sense in which the middle class has been aware of its interests, and they have not been perceived to be altogether akin to the working class or a recognition of opposition to upper-class economic dominance. Periodic pique is generated by "corporate rip-offs" and large corporate profits, but so too is there animosity over labour unions, despite growing middle-class union participation. For the securely employed blue- or white-collar worker, there is as yet no fundamental dissatisfaction with the existing system of economic distribution. Only the agriculturalist seems under severe pressure and threatening radical action, as would be in their long tradition.

The Impoverished

The unemployed and marginally employed are not a significant force for change, cut off as they are from organization, and sustained in their subordination by welfare programs. The welfare state effectively pacifies deprived individuals, unless their ranks are drastically enlarged by persons previously enjoying superior economic advantage.

Piven and Cloward (1971) have proposed that the history of welfare policy in the United States is one of response to successive economic crises. We might consider Canadian government welfare responses to the depression of the 1930s, and currently to inflation and unemployment, as such. They are not policies that alter the distribution of resources or the structure of class, but stabilize it. As one not so radical group (the Senate Committee on Poverty) put it, the welfare system "has treated the symptoms of poverty and left the disease itself untouched." (Canada, 1971: xv.) But the programs were not designed to do otherwise. Moreover, the stabilization is secured using revenues in large part obtained from the wage and salary makers, rather than from business, thereby in no way challenging the economic dominance of the ruling class. In a period of inflation and rising welfare costs, corporations in Canada reported record profits in 1973.

Welfare programs, or in the current euphemism favoured by the Economic Council of Canada, "transfer payments to individuals",

Figure 5-1
*Proposed Federal Government Expenditures,
According to Functions, for 1973-74*

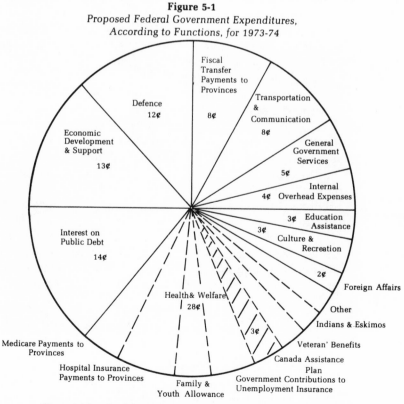

The graph is based on information provided in the Treasury Board Report *How Your Tax Dollar Is Spent 1973-74*, published by Information Canada, Ottawa 1973. Prepared by Nadya Tarasoff, Social Planning Council of Ottawa and District. (Tarasoff, 1973: 3)

Figure 5-2

Provincial Government of Ontario Expenditures for Fiscal Year 1971-72

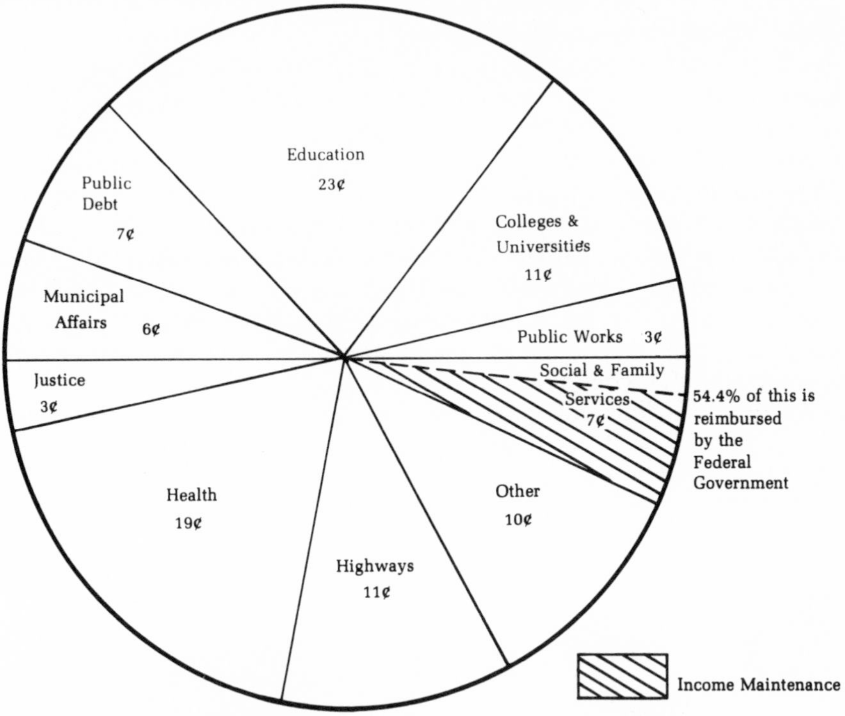

The graph is based on information provided in *The Public Accounts 1971-72*, Volume 1 — Financial Statements, Province of Ontario, printed and published by the Queen's Printer and Publisher, Toronto 1972. Prepared by Nadya Tarasoff, Social Planning Council of Ottawa and District. (Tarasoff, 1973: 4)

amount to taking from the not-so-poor and not-so-rich and giving to the utterly deprived. But only giving a little to the deprived; most of it comes back to the middle class. The taxes that support such "transfer payments" are paid by employees. In 1970 over 80 per cent of total income taxes in Canada were collected from persons earning under $20 000 per year. More startling, 41.6 per cent of total taxes were paid by persons earning between $5 000 and $10 000. (Tarasoff, 1973: 1.) When indirect taxes are also considered, such as those on clothing and all consumer items, we have all the more clearly regressive rather than progressive tax systems, insofar as the taxes paid by low-income persons constitute a far greater proportion of their income than for higher-income persons, particularly those enjoying business profits rather than wages or salaries.

Most of these tax revenues then benefit the middle class, further indicative of the essential stability or maintenance of the system. For 1973-74, projected federal spending of tax revenues only involves 28 cents of the tax dollar for "health and welfare", and an additional 13 cents for "economic development and support". (Tarasoff, 1973.) And much of this goes to middle- and upper-class persons, not only insofar as they receive profits from economic development schemes, but also in that "health and welfare" spending includes medicare payments and hospital insurance payments to the provinces, family allowances, and veterans' allowances. (Figure 5-1.) A similar pattern of redistribution operates at the provincial level, as Ontario data illustrate (Figure 5-2).

Generally, therefore, present government systems act to reinforce the class structure and what could be called "false consciousness". Wage earners are taxed, where corporate profits are relatively unscathed. The taxes then are returned as benefits to wage earners. The extremes of wealth and poverty are not seriously affected, except for some necessary support of the impoverished, which, however humane, also serves to enhance the dependency relations of the recipients and gloss over the persistence of disparities. There is no significant redistribution of wealth, but only a circular distribution.

Change

Barring a major economic catastrophe or some external intervention, there is little prospect of drastic change in the Canadian class structure. The ruling class is not apt to undertake the erosion of its advantages, the middle and working classes are entwined in a feedback system of affluent short-term economic competition, and the destitute are restrained in a web of welfare dependency. A proletarian consciousness consisting of an organized and effective opposition to the ruling stratum is improbable under existing conditions of competitive economic gamesmanship. In his optimism Mills offered the new famous remark that, "Because men are not 'class conscious' at all times and in all places does not mean that 'there are no classes' or that 'in America everybody is middle class.' " (Mills, 1951: 294.) But neither is it true that because men are class conscious sometimes, and because classes are real, that class contestation of a magnitude sufficient to realize structural change is likely.

The wage and salary workers contain the potential for political action, but it is not a potential apt to crystallize without a major catalyst. Economic breakdown of the like of the 1930s, which economists confidently assure us is impossible, would be such a crisis. Conceivably nationalist movements in Canada could also serve politicizing class actions. However, there is certainly no assurance that it would be action to the "left", and in aid of a more egalitarian society.

Johnson has argued that Canada has experienced a decline in the size and influence of the petite bourgeoisie — that is, small businessmen and farmers. In the past, he argues, such persons have been in opposition to the working class, a statement not altogether correct in light of periodic working-class-farm alliance in Saskatchewan. But in the deterioration of their positions he suggests that perhaps there has been a polarization of class interests. (Johnson, 1972.) Similarly, Clement has argued that there has been a crystallization of class interests insofar as the capitalist élite in Canada has become more exclusive and difficult of entry. (Clement, 1975.) The validity of the arguments rests on a number of assumptions, not the least of which relates to the character of labour and white-collar action. Labour organized in international unions has always been very moderate in ideology and action, and salaried workers have always been conservative. (Mills, 1951.) The middle class has replaced the small entrepreneur or petite bourgeoisie in our stratification system, growing from 15.2 per cent of the labour force in 1901 to 38.8 per cent in 1961. (Meltz, 1969.) This group mediates now between the owners and the working class; should it become radicalized in its union relations to its employers, then the polarization of which Johnson speaks may be realized. But it seems a tenuous hope, especially in light of the increasing entry of women into the labour force, constituting a new group to be "educated" to class consciousness.

Regional Opposition and Change

Class-related hostility in all probability will continue to be most viably expressed under regional differences. The regions in Canada have distinct interests and identities. Particularly as they move effectively to develop in competition with central Canada, class conflict will be manifest in regional conflict. The so-called rise of the middle class in Quebec (Guindon, 1969), a feature of industrial development and urbanization in Quebec, has led to a vigorous separatist movement by the middle class, with organized labour support, who view their interests in opposition to Anglophone Canada. Similarly, one may predict a surge of western Canadian separatism as the western provinces, exploiting the capital generated by sales of oil and natural gas, will move to industrialize and compete with eastern Canada in secondary production. Given the ideological convictions of the separatists in Quebec, which in large degree are socialist, and similarly, given the radical tradition of the West and the well-established N.D.P. socialist power base, we could expect such regional separatist efforts to emphasize and to some extent realize a redistribution of economic resources in amelioration of class distinctions. At the same time Ontario, and probably the Maritimes, would remain relatively unaltered in social structure. As the theory of relative deprivation would suggest, those regions that have and are experiencing developmental changes are those wherein deprivation will be perceived as salient and prompt social action. To put it crudely, central Ontario is on top, the Maritimes on the bottom, and the West and Quebec are the middle class who are apt to incite the Canadian middle-class revolution and perhaps along the way seriously alter the basic structure of inequality in Canada. But to count on the influence of such separatist movements, and to further expect that they would necessarily make for autonomous or semi-autonomous political entities that are more egalitarian than the present Canadian federal system, is to engage in fragile speculation. At best we could predict some redistribution of wealth in the nation, and perhaps some burst of iedological idealism in the midst of the separatist zeal — a zeal, however, that could also justify excesses.

Generally, it is probable that the basic structure of class in Canadian society will change little in the near future. The ruling class is well established, and the centre party, the Liberals, as well as the opposition parties, the Conservatives and the N.D.P., seem as committed as the Liberals to variations on the theme of "welfarism" rather than fundamental structural change. Policies that would alter the inheritance of unequal resources and opportunities do not seem imminent; rather, present and anticipated policies emphasize variations on existing patterns of ownership and taxation and caring for Canadians through welfare programs, thereby tolerating and reinforcing the class system.

The rituals of conventional politics are limited to such a conception. Effective challenge to this conventional politics may to some extent come from regional movements, as has been the case historically. And it will come in some part from the activities of trade unions. But failing a class polarization, which we have already suggested is improbable, effective change in the stratification system is not imminent.

Only some issue or event that will challenge the present conventional welfare-related political opportunities is apt to challenge the existing stratification system. Hence our reference to regional separatism, and perhaps also nationalist opposition to foreign economic control, serving as foci of radical action, even though these issues are themselves readily conventionalized. But in the meanwhile, the privileged enjoy their advantage, and the underprivileged suffer the "structural violence" inherent in Canada's system of institutionalized inequalities.

Conclusions

Processes of social control and socialization render social systems and their patterns of privilege remarkably resistant to fundamental change. There is no human precedent that would lead one to expect a ruling class to divest itself of power and privilege. We have seen that the Canadian ruling class is well established and effectively in control of conventional politics in Canada. Their position is only likely to be altered by the action of less privileged strata in Canadian society. But that action is unlikely. In reading a recent prize-winning book that develops a devastating critique of welfare policies in the United States, one wonders how the authors could finally conclude by suggesting more welfare. (Piven and Cloward, 1971: 347.) Their reason now seems obvious; in the face of the improbability of basic economic reform and change in the class structure, welfare, despite an admission of the evil of class society, is at least humane. But it is not even an approximation of a redistribution of wealth and opportunity sufficient to realize the ideal of minimal stratification.

Some would place their expectations of change in the prospect of extreme and perhaps violent class conflicts; from such crises, rather than from the ritual of everyday politics, would change emerge. Canadian society has experienced numerous instances of overt class conflict, often including acts of violence. These do indicate the reality of class relations and of class consciousness. In that sense, such conflict is a normal feature of class stratification and not mere aberration.

But it is also the case that class confrontations have become ritualized or institutionalized. Violent opposition will periodically occur as it always has in Canada, but labour relations with owners and government have become conventional and restricted to short-term economic bargaining after the American fashion of establishment labour action. Wealth is not really redistributed in Canadian society, such as to challenge the viability of classes. Nor are there serious demands for such redistribution. Rather the circulation of economic resources is within the parameters of the class structure and reinforces it.

There are stubborn theoretical projections of prospects for increased class consciousness and action. These characteristically have resorted to the proletarization of the middle class and the polarization of the class structure. (Mills, 1951: 301-350; Lockwood, 1958; Johnson, 1972; Clement, 1975.) There is some plausibility to such arguments, but also a large dose of wishful thinking. Resort to union organization and tactics of bargaining by the middle class overemphasizes the proportion of such middle-class unionization, but more fundamental, misjudges the goals of such activity. We judge them to be of the order of conventional non-disruptive politics, and bargaining for short-term economic gain, as labour-owner relations generally in Canada.

It seems, therefore, that prospects for considerable and rapid change in Canada's class structure are improbable. Unless one is prepared to trust in a radical variant of "aristocratic responsibility", the ruling class is not likely to institute far-reaching social changes, but only an elaboration of welfare as crisis-response. Given the history of Canadian protest politics, we could expect demands for change increasingly to be associated with regional identities, in particular Quebec and the Canadian West, the latter perhaps bifurcated between the Prairies and the west coast. As these regions experience greater economic gains, their perception of relative deprivation vis-á-vis Ontario industrial interests is likely to promote more vigorous demands, which could realize a redistribution of advantage somewhat affecting classes. This would, however, only really be significant if the regional contestation were itself radicalized, because of federal opposition and because of ideological inputs; the prospects of Quebec separatism seem most likely to be of this sort. But such radicalization cannot be predicted to be necessarily in the direction of egalitarian principles, insofar as seeking minimal stratification, but rather, is apt to amount to mere regional redeployment of advantage, to the benefit of regional privileged populations. Generally, regional action is even more probably to remain within the context of conventional provincial-federal negotiations, and the alteration in the distribution of advantage amounting only to an altered geographical concentration, and not an altered class distribution.

So the concluding irony might be this: only cataclysm is likely to precipitate fundamental change in the Canadian class structure. Only in disaster will the stratification system be altered, and thereby the cost of the egalitarian society would be high. Short of that, the probable outcome of evolutionary development in Canada will be an elaboration of welfarism, meritocracy for the middle class, and pre-eminent privilege for the ruling minority. Assuming its validity, the reader may find the conclusion consoling or disturbing.

Bibliography

Abella, Irving, *Nationalism, Communism, and Canadian Labour*, Toronto: University of Toronto Press, 1973.

Adorno, T.W.; Frenkel-Brunswik Else; Levinson, D.J.; and Sanford, R.N. *The Authoritarian Personality*, New York: Harper, 1950.

Alford, R. *Party and Society*, Chicago: Aldine Publishing Co., 1963.

Alford, R. "The Social Bases of Political Cleavage in 1962" in J. Meisel (ed.) *Papers on the 1962 Election*, Toronto: University of Toronto Press, 1964.

Alford, R. "Class Voting in the Anglo-American Political Systems" in S.M. Lipset and S. Rokkan (eds.), *Party Systems and Voter Alignments*, New York: The Free Press, 1967, 67-93.

Allingham, John. "Religious Affiliation and Social Class in Ontario", Hamilton: M.A. thesis, Department of Sociology, McMaster University, May 1962.

Anderson, Charles, *The Political Economy of Social Class*, Englewood Cliffs, N.J.: Prentice-Hall Inc., 1974.

Anderson, Grace, "Voting Behaviour and the Ethnic-Religions Variable: A Study of a Federal Election in Hamilton, Ontario", *Canadian Journal of Economics and Political Science* xxxii, (1966) 27-37.

Badgley, Robin F., and Wolfe, Samuel. *Doctor's Strike: Medical Care and Conflict in Saskatchewan*, Toronto: Macmillan of Canada, 1967.

Balawyder, A. *The Winnipeg General Strike*, Vancouver, Toronto, Montreal: The Copp Clark Pub. Co., 1967.

Beattie, C., and Spencer, B. "Career Attainment in Canadian Bureaucracies: Unscrambling the Effects of Age, Seniority, Education and Ethnolinguistic Factors", *AJS* 77, (1971) 472-490.

Beattie, Christopher. *Minority Men in a Majority Setting*, Toronto: McClelland and Stewart (The Carleton Library), 1975.

Bell, C. and Newby, H. *Community Studies*, London: George Allen and Unwin Ltd., 1971.

Bennett, John. *Hutterite Brethren: The Agricultural Economy and Social Organization of a Communal People*, Stanford: Stanford University Press, 1967.

Bennett, John W., *Northern Plainsman: Adaptive Strategy and Agrarian Life*, Chicago: Aldine Publishing Co., 1969.

Bennett, J., and Krueger, C. "Agrarian Pragmatism and Radical Politics" in S.M. Lipset, *Agrarian Socialism* (new ed., Part 2), Berkeley: University of California Press, 1968, 347-363.

Blishen, Bernard. "Social Class and Opportunity in Canada", *CRSA* 17, (1970) 110-127.

Boroway, Alan. "Indian Poverty in Canada" in J. Harp and J. Hofley. (eds.) *Poverty in Canada*, Scarborough: Prentice-Hall of Canada, 1971, 213-218.

Bottomore, T.B. *Classes in Modern Society*, London: George Allen and Unwin, 1965.

Brown, L., and Brown, C. *An Unauthorized History of the RCMP*, Toronto: James Lewis and Samuel, 1973.

Burbidge, Scott. "Structural Factors and Occupational Mobility: A Study of Parental and Peer Group Influences on the Career Patterns of Lower Class Males." Halifax: M.A. Thesis, Department of Sociology, Dalhousie University, April 1965.

Canada, *Illness and Health Care in Canada: Canadian Sickness Survey, 1950-51*, Ottawa: Queen's Printer, 1960.

Canada, *Selected Statistics on Children*, Ottawa: Queen's Printer, 1965.

Canada, *Report of the Royal Commission on Bilingualism and Biculturalism (Book III, The Work World)*, Ottawa: Queen's Printer, 1969.

Canada, *Earnings of Dentists in Canada, 1959-1968*, Ottawa, Queen's Printer: 1970.

Canada, Poverty in Canada; *Report of the Special Senate Committee on Poverty*. Ottawa: Information Canada, 1971.

Canada, *Household Facilities by Income and Other Characteristics for 1968*, Ottawa: Information Canada, 1972.

Canada, *Canada Year Book 1972*, Ottawa: Information Canada, 1972A.

Canada, *Perspective Canada: A Compendium of Social Statistics*, Ottawa: Information Canada, 1974.

Chapin, F.S. "A Quantitative Scale for Rating of the Home and Social Environment of Middle Class Families in an Urban Environment". *Journal of Educational Psychology*, 19, (1928) 99-111.

Chapin, F.S. *Measurement of Social Status by the Use of the Social Status Scale*, Minnesota: University of Minnesota Press, 1933.

Clark, S.D. "Foreword" in D.C. Masters, *The Winnipeg General Strike*, Toronto: University of Toronto Press, 1950, i-x.

Clark, S.D. *The Suburban Society*, Toronto: University of Toronto Press, 1966.

Clark, S.D. "The Position of the French-Speaking Population in Northern Industrial Communities" in R. Ossenberg (ed) *Canadian Society: Pluralism, Change and Conflict*, Scarborough: Prentice-Hall of Canada, 1971, 62-85.

Clement, Wallace. "Parasites, Satellites, and Stratification", Ottawa: Department of Sociology and Anthropology, Carleton University, February 1973 (mimeo).

Clement, Wallace, "The Social Origins of the Industrial Elite, 1885-1910", Ottawa: Carleton University, 1973 a. (mimeo).

Clement, W., and Olsen, D. "Official Ideology and Ethnic Power: Canadian Elites, 1953-1973", Montreal: Meetings of the ASA, August 1974 (mimeo).

Clement, Wallace, *The Canadian Corporate Elite: Economic Power in Canada*, Toronto: McClelland and Stewart (The Carleton Library), 1975.

Collins, John. "Trader Trudeau", Montreal: *The Gazette*, Wednesday, March 27, 1974, p.5.

Creighton, Donald, *Canada's First Century*, Toronto: Macmillan of Canada, 1972.

Crysdale, Stewart. "Occupational and Social Mobility in Riverdale, A Blue Collar Community", Toronto: Ph.D. thesis, Department of Sociology, University of Toronto, March 1968.

Crysdale, S., and Beattie, C. *Sociology Canada: An Introductory Text*. Toronto: Butterworth and Co. Ltd., 1973.

Curtis, James, and Scott, William (eds.). *Social Stratification in Canada*, Scarborough: Prentice-Hall of Canada, 1973.

Dahrendorf, Ralf, *Class and Class Conflict in Industrial Society*, Stanford: Stanford University Press, 1959.

Davidson, H., and Lang, G. "Children's Perceptions of their Teachers' Feelings Towards Them Related to Self-Perception, School Achievement, and Behaviour", *Journal of Experimental Education*, 29 (1960), 107-118.

Darroch, A., and Marston, W. "The Social Class Basis of Ethnic Residential Segregation: The Canadian Case", *AJS*, 77 (1971), 491-510.

Davis, Arthur K. "Canadian Society and History as Hinterland Versus Metropolis" in R. Ossenberg (ed.), *Canadian Society: Pluralism, Change and Conflict*, Scarborough: Prentice-Hall of Canada, 1971, pp. 6-32.

Davis, Kingsley, and Moore, Wilbert E. "Some Principles of Stratification", *ASR* 10 (April, 1945), 242-249.

Dawson, R., and Prewitt, K. *Political Socialization*, Boston: Little, Brown and Co., 1969.

Djilas, Milovan. *The New Class*, New York: Frederick A. Praeger, 1957.

Drucker, Philip. *Cultures of the North Pacific Coast*, San Francisco: Chandler Publishing Co., 1965.

Ewing, Anthony. "Social Class and Voting in Vancouver Civic Elections", Ottawa: M.A. thesis, Department of Sociology and Anthropology, Carleton University, 1972.

Forcese, D., and Siemens, L.B. *School-Related Factors and the Aspiration Levels of Manitoba Senior High School Students*, Winnipeg: Faculty of Agriculture and Home Economics, University of Manitoba, 1965.

Forcese, D.; Richer, S.; de Vries, J.; and McRoberts, H. "The Methodology of a Crisis Survey", St. John's, Nfld.; Meetings of the Canadian Sociology and Anthropology Association, June, 1971 (mimeo).

Forcese, D., and de Vries, J. "Occupational and Electoral Success in Canada: The 1972 Federal Election", Ottawa: Carleton University, 1974.

Forcese, D., and Richer, S. (contrib. eds.). *Issues in Canadian Society: An Introduction to Sociology*, Scarborough: Prentice-Hall of Canada, 1975.

Fraser, Howard, "Socio-economic Status, Morbidity, and the Utilization of Health Resources of Calgary", Calgary: M.A. thesis, Department of Sociology, University of Calgary, 1968.

Garcia, John, "I.Q.: The Conspiracy", *Psychology Today* 6 (Sept. 1972), pp. 40-92, 92-97.

Gilbert, S., and McRoberts, H. "Differentiation and Stratification: The Issue of Inequality" in D. Forcese and S. Richer (contrib. eds.), *Issues in Canadian Society: An Introduction to Sociology*, Scarborough: Prentice-Hall of Canada, 1975.

Gilbert, Sid, "Educational and Occupational Aspirations of Ontario High School Students: A Multivariate Analysis", Ottawa: Ph.D. thesis, Department of Sociology and Anthropology, Carleton University, 1973.

Gilbert, Sid, and McRoberts, Hugh. "Academic Stratification and Educational Plans: A Reassessment", Winnipeg and Ottawa: July 1974 (mimeo).

Glass, D.V. *Social Mobility in Britain*, London: Routledge and Kegan Paul, 1945.

Gockel, G. "Income and Religious Affiliation: A Regression Analysis", *AJS* 74 (1969), 632-47.

Goodall, Raymond, "Religious Style, and Social Class", Vancouver: M.A. thesis, Dept. of Sociology, University of British Columbia, May 1970.

Gouldner, Alvin, *The Coming Crisis of Western Sociology*, New York: Avon Books, 1971.

Gray, James, *The Winter Years*, Toronto: Macmillan of Canada, 1966.

Guindon, Hubert, "Social Unrest, Social Class, and Quebec's Bureaucratic Revolution", *Queen's Quarterly* LXXI (1964), 150-162.

Guttman, Louis, "A Revision of Chapin's Social Status Scale". *ASR* 7 (1942), 362-69.

Hall, Oswald, "The Canadian Division of Labour Revisited" in J. Curtis and W. Scott (eds.) *Social Stratification in Canada*, Scarborough: Prentice-Hall of Canada, 1973, pp. 46-54.

Harp, John, and Hofley, John, eds. *Poverty in Canada*. Scarborough: Prentice-Hall of Canada, 1971.

Heap, James (ed.). *Everybody's Canada: The Vertical Mosaic Reviewed and Re-examined*, Toronto: Burns and MacEachern, 1974.

Hoar, Victor, "Introduction" in R. Liversedge, *Recollections of the On to Ottawa Trek*, Toronto: McClelland and Stewart, 1973, pp. VII-XVIII.

Hoare, Michael, "Social Origins of Nurses and Career Satisfaction". A Study of Student Nurses in Three Metropolitan Halifax Schools of Nursing". Halifax: M.A. thesis, Dept. of Sociology, Dalhousie University, 1969.

Horowitz, Gad, *Canadian Labour in Politics*, Toronto: University of Toronto Press, 1968.

Hughes, Everett. *French Canada in Transition*, Chicago: University of Chicago Press, 1943.

Hunter, Floyd, *Community Power Structure*, Chapel Hill: University of North Carolina Press, 1952.

Jackson, J.E.W., and Poushinsky, N. *Migration to Northern Mining Communities: Structural and Social-Psychological Dimensions*, Winnipeg: Center for Settlement Studies, University of Manitoba, 1971.

Jansen, Clifford, "The Italian Community in Toronto" in Jean Elliott (ed.) *Minority Canadians: Immigrant Groups*, Scarborough: Prentice-Hall of Canada, 1971.

Johnson, Leo A. "The Development of Class in Canada in the Twentieth Century" in Gary Teeple (ed.), *Capitalism and the National Question in Canada*, Toronto: University of Toronto Press, 1972, 141-183.

Jones, Frank, "The Social Origins of High School Teachers in a Canadian City". *CJEPS* XXIX (Nov. 1963), 529-35.

Kerchoff, Alan, *Socialization and Social Class*, Englewood Cliffs: Prentice-Hall, 1972.

Kerr, Donald, "Metropolitan Dominance in Canada" in John Warkentin (ed.), *Canada, A Geographical Interpretation*, Toronto: Methuen, 1970.

Kluckhomn, F., and Strodtbeck, F. *Variations in Value Orientation*, Evanston, Illinois: Row, Peterson, 1961.

Langton, Kenneth, *Political Socialization*, New York: Oxford University Press, 1969.

Laskin, Richard, *Organizations in a Saskatchewan Town*, Saskatoon: Center for Community Studies, Nov. 1961.

Lenski, Gerhard E. *Power and Privilege*, New York: McGraw-Hill Book Co., 1966.

Lipset, Seymour M. *Agrarian Socialism*, Berkeley: University of California Press, 1950.

Lipset, Seymour M. *The First New Nation*, New York: Basic Books, 1963.

Lipset, Seymour M. *Political Man*, Garden City, N.Y.: Doubleday and Co., 1965.

Lipset, Seymour M. *Agrarian Socialism* (rev. ed.). Garden City, N.Y.: Doubleday and Co. 1968.

Liversedge, Ronald, *Recollections of the On to Ottawa Trek* (ed. by V. Hoar). Toronto: McClelland and Stewart Ltd. (The Carleton Library), 1973

Lockwood, David, *The Blackcoated Worker*, London: Unwin University Books, 1958.

Lorimer, J., and Phillips, M. *Working People: Life in a Downtown City Neighbourhood*, Toronto: James Lewis and Samuel Ltd., 1971.

Lucas, Rex, *Minetown, Milltown, Railtown: Life in Canadian Communities of Single Industry*, Toronto: University of Toronto Press, 1971.

Lynd, R.S., and Lynd, H.M. *Middletown: A Study in Modern American Culture*, New York: Harcourt, Brace and World, 1929.

Lynd, R.S., and Lynd, H.M. *Middletown in Transition*, New York: Harcourt, Brace and World, 1937.

Manzer, R. *Canada: A Socio-Political Report*, Toronto: McGraw-Hill Ryerson, 1974.

Marx, Karl, and Engels, Friedrich, *The Communist Manifesto* (ed. and Intro. by R. Pascal). New York: International Publishers, 1947.

Marx, Karl, and Engels, Friedrich, *The German Ideology*, Parts I and III (ed. and intro. by R. Pascal). New York: International Publishers, 1947.

Masters, D.C. *The Winnipeg General Strike*, Toronto: University of Toronto Press, 1950.

Matthiasson, J. "Resident Mobility in Resource Frontier Communities" in John Matthiasson (ed.), *Two Studies on Fort McMurray*, Winnipeg: Center for Settlement Studies, University of Manitoba, 1971.

Mayer, K. and Buckley, W., *Class and Society* (3rd ed.). New York: Random House, 1969.

McCrorie, James N. "Change and Paradox in Agrarian Social Movements: The Case of Saskatchewan" in R. Ossenberg (eds.), *Canadian Society: Pluralism, Change, and Conflict*, Scarborough: Prentice-Hall of Canada, 1971, pp. 36-51.

McKenzie, R., and Silver, A. "The Delicate Experiment: Industrialism, Conservatism, and Working-Class Tories in England" in S.M. Lipset and S. Rokkan (eds.), *Party Systems and Voter Alignments*, New York: The Free Press, 1967, pp. 115-125.

McNaught, Kenneth, "Violence in Canadian History" in John Moir (ed.), *Character and Circumstance*, Toronto: Macmillan of Canada, 1970, pp. 66-84.

McRoberts, Hugh A. "Follow-up of Grade 12 Students from the Blishen Porter Study of Educational Aspirations". Ottawa: Dept. of Sociology and Anthropology, Carleton University, 1973.

Meltz, Noah, *Manpower in Canada, 1931-1961*, Ottawa: Queen's Printer, 1969.

Merton, Robert K. *Social Theory and Social Structure*, New York: The Free Press, 1957.

Michels, Robert, *Political Parties: A Sociological Study on the Oligarchical Tendencies of Modern Democracy* (trans. by E. Paul and C. Paul). New York: Collier Books, 1962.

Milbrath, Lester, *Political Participation*: Chicago, Rand McNally and Co., 1965.

Miliband, Ralph, *The State in Capitalist Society*, New York: Basic Books, 1969.

Mills, C. Wright, *White Collar*, New York: Oxford University Press, 1951.

Mills, C.W.*The Power Elite*, New York: Oxford University Press, 1956.

Morton, W.L. *The Progressive Party in Canada*, Toronto: University of Toronto Press, 1950.

Mosca, Gaetano, *The Ruling Class* (ed. and rev. by A. Livingston, trans. by H. Kahn). New York: McGraw-Hill Book Co., 1939.

Myers, Gustavus, *A History of Canadian Wealth*, Toronto: James Lewis and Samuel, 1972.

National Opinion Research Center, "Jobs and Occupation: A Popular Evaluation", *Public Opinion News* 9 (1974), 3-13.

Neatby, H. Blair, *The Politics of Chaos: Canada in the Thirties*, Toronto: Macmillan of Canada, 1972.

Or, Michael, "A Comparison of High School Graduates and Dropouts in Halifax", Halifax: M.A. thesis, Department of Sociology, Dalhousie University, 1970.

Ossenberg, Richard, "Social Pluralism in Quebec: Continuity Change and Conflict" in R. Ossenberg (ed.), *Canadian Society: Pluralism, Change, and Conflict*, Scarborough: Prentice-Hall of Canada, pp. 103-123.

Penner, Norman (ed.). *Winnipeg 1919*, Toronto: James Lewis and Samuel, 1973.

Peters, Victor, *All Things Common*, Winnipeg: The University of Manitoba Press, 1965.

Pike, Robert, *Who Doesn't get to University and Why*, Ottawa: Association of Universities and Colleges of Canada, 1970.

Pinard, Maurice, "Working Class Politics: An Interpretation of the Quebec Case", *CRSA* 7 (1970), 87-109.

Piven, A., and Cloward, R. *Regulating the Poor*, New York: Pantheon Books, 1971.

Podoluk, Jenny, *Incomes of Canadians*, Ottawa, Dominion Bureau of Statistics, 1968.

Porter, John, "The Concentration of Economic Power and the Economic Elite in Canada", *CJEPS* XXII (May 1956), 199-220.

Porter, John, *Canadian Social Structure: A Statistical Profile*, Toronto: McClelland and Stewart (The Carleton Library), 1967.

Porter, John, *The Vertical Mosaic*, Toronto: University of Toronto Press, 1965.

Porter, John, *Canadian Social Structure: A Statistical Profile*, Toronto: McClelland and Stewart (The Carleton Library), 1967.

Porter, John, "Politics and Minorities: Canada and The United States", Michigan: Intercollegiate Conference in Canadian American Relations, Michigan State University, Feb. 1968 (mimeo).

Presthus, Robert, *Elite Accomodation in Canadian Politics*, Toronto: Macmillan of Canada, 1973.

Presthus, Robert, *Elites in the Policy Process*, London: Cambridge University Press, 1974.

Rainwater, Lee (ed.), *Inequality and Justice*, Chicago: Aldine Publishing Co., 1974.

Rennie, Douglas, "The Ethnic Division of Labour in Montreal from 1931-1951", Montreal: M.A. thesis, Department of Sociology, McGill University, 1953.

Rioux, Marcel, *Quebec in Question*, Toronto: James Lewis and Samuel, 1971.

Robin, Martin, *Radical Politics and Canadian Labour 1880-1930*, Kingston: Queen's University, 1968.

Rocher, Guy, "Formal Education: The Issue of Opportunity" in S. Richer, D. Forcese, *Issues in Canadian Society: An Introduction to Sociology*, Scarborough: Prentice-Hall of Canada, 1975.

Russell, George, "Bound Together in the Fear of a Harsh God". *Weekend Magazine*, April 6, 1974, pp. 2-10.

Siemens, Leonard B., and Jackson, J.E. *Educational Plans and Their Fulfillment: A Study of Selected High School Students in Manitoba*, Winnipeg: Faculty of Agriculture and Home Economics, University of Manitoba, 1965.

Siemens, L.B. *Single Enterprise Community Studies in Northern Canada*, Winnipeg: Center for Settlement Studies, University of Manitoba, 1973.

Smith, Joel, Melting-Pot-Mosaic: Consideration for a Prognosis", Michigan: Intercollegiate Conference of Canadian-American Relations, Michigan State University, Feb. 1968 (mimeo).

Stone, Leroy O. *Migration in Canada: Some Regional Aspects*, Ottawa: Dominion Bureau of Statistics, 1969.

Stub, Holger (ed.). *Status Groups in Modern Society: Alternatives to Class Analysis*, New York: Dryden Press, 1972, pp. 1-6.

Svalastoga, Kaare, *Social Differentiation*, New York: David McKay Co., 1965.

Tarasoff, Nadya, "Some Notes on 'Government Transfer Payments To Individuals' ", Ottawa: Social Planning Council of Ottawa, Nov. 28, 1973 (mimeo).

Teeple, Gary, "Land, Labour, and Capital in Pre-Confederation Canada" in Gary Teeple (ed.), *Capitalism and the National Question in Canada*, Toronto: University of Toronto Press, 1972. 43-66.

Teevan Jr., James J., and Jackson, J.E. Winston "Religion and Social Class in Toronto", Montreal: Meetings of the Canadian Sociology and Anthropology Associations, June 1972 (mimeo).

Thoenes, Piet, *The Elite in the Welfare State*, London: Faber and Faber, 1966.

Ward, Norman, *The Canadian House of Commons: Representation*. Toronto: University of Toronto Press, 1950.

Warner, W. Lloyd, and Lunt, P.S. *The Status System of a Modern Community*, New Haven: Yale University Press, 1947.

Warner W. Lloyd (with M. Meeker and K. Eells). *Social Class In America: The Evaluation of Status*, New York: Science Research Associates, 1949.

Weber, Max, *From Max Weber* (trans. by H. Gerth and C.W. Mills), New York: Oxford University Press, 1958.

Weyer, E.M. *The Eskimos: Their Environment and Folkways*, New Haven: Yale University Press, 1932.

Wichern, P.H. *Two Studies in Political Development on Canada's Resource Frontier*, Winnipeg: Center for Settlement Studies, University of Manitoba, 1972.

INDEX

Abella, Irving, 117, 118
Aberhardt, William, 102, 107
achievement, 21, by class, 74; differential, 74; educational, 74 — (of male non-agricultural labour force, 80); inherited, 67; occupational, 68, 74; political, 51
action, social, vii
activities, industrial, 41; primary, 41
Adorno, T.W., 94
advantage(s) 3, class, 26; distribution of, 129; maintenance of upper class, 74; social, measurement of, 73; socio-economic, 61
affluence, 33
Africa, 47
age, 9
agriculturists, corporate, 9
Alberta, 8, 9, 102; regional stratification, 37
Alford, R., 96, 97, 98, 106
aliens, 115; deportation of, 112
All Canadian Congress of Labour (1927), 117
allegiance, 25
Allingham, John, 105
"amenities", by region, 37-8
"American Dream", 1
American Federation of Labour, 117
American Republic, 1
American Revolution (1775-81), 57
American unions, 117-18; American based in Canada, 122
American, "wild west", 57
Americans, 50
Amish, 8
Anderson, Charles, 2, 18, 51
Anderson, Grace, 106
Anglo-Canadians, 31, 33-4
Anglophone, 49; Canada, 58, 127; influence, 58
"aristocratic compact", 41
ascription, 21, 58, 81; inequality by, 5; inheritance, 11; rank, 11
aspirations, educational, 68-9; high, 90; inherited, 67; occupational, 70; to status of father, 69, 71-2; varies by class, 70, 74; varies with region, 69, 70
Atlantic Provinces, 24, 32
Atlantic Region, 29
attainment, educational, 52; of labour force, 64-5; university, of population, 65
attitudes, class, differences in, 68; of young people, 68; of teachers, 71
Australia, election in, 97
"authoritarianism", 94

awards, honorific, 20; material, 20
awareness, 27; class, 25, 55; group, 19; material, 25

backgrounds, British Canadian, 78, 80; Jewish, 78, 80
Badgley, Robin F., 120-21
Balawyder, A., 115, 116-17
banks, 50; control of, 42
bargaining, economic, 129; organized, 122; short-term, 129
Beattie, C., 46, 51, 107
Beattie, Christopher, 46
Beckett, Archbishop Thomas (1118-70), 12
behaviour, 3, 4, 8, 27, 29, 58, 75, 82-109; attitudes influencing, 68; class, in relation to religion, 104; deviant, 90; influence of religious training, 107; lower class, political, 94; motivating of, 19; non-conventional, 103; non-interest, related to religious ideology, 108; political, 94, 98, — (affected by religion, 106); uniformity of, 5; vices, 91; violation of property rights, 91; violent or aggressive, 93
Bennett, J., 103
Bennett, John, 8
Bennett, John W., 8, 28, 29
Bennett, Richard Bedford (1870-1947), 119, 120
Berton, Pierre (1920-   ), 26
bias, class, 51, 68; ethnic, 52, 112 — (enters educational achievement, 78)
Biggar, Sask., voluntary associations, 30
bilingualism, 46
Blau, Peter, 18
Blishen, Bernard R., 18, 35, 47, 48, 72, 73, 76-7
"Bloody Saturday", 116
Bolshevism, 115
Borden, Sir Robert Laird (1854-1937), 116
Boroway, Alan, 55
Bottomore, T.B., 2
Brandon, Man., 35
Briant, P., 43
British, 50
British Columbia, Prov. of, 4, 112; poverty in, 35; regional stratification, 37
British North America, 26
Brown, C., 112, 114
Brown, L., 112, 114
Buckley, W., 12, 13
bureaucracy, federal, ethnic representation, 51
business, men of power in, 49

137